D0891886

BULLEIT PROOF

How I Took a
150-Year-Old
Family Recipe
and a Revolver,
and Disrupted
the Entire
Liquor Industry

BULLEIT PROOF

One Bottle,
One Sip,
One Handshake
at a Time

TOM BULLEIT | WITH ALAN EISENSTOCK

WILEY

Published by John Wiley & Sons, Inc., Hoboken, New Jersey.

Published simultaneously in Canada.

For general information on our other products and services or for technical support, please contact our Customer Care Department within the United States at (800) 762–2974, outside the United States at (317) 572–3993 or fax (317) 572–4002.

Wiley publishes in a variety of print and electronic formats an   d by print-on-demand. Some material included with standard print versions of this book may not be included in e-books or in print-on-demand. If this book refers to media such as a CD or DVD that is not included in the version you purchased, you may download this material at http://booksupport.wiley.com. For more information about Wiley products, visit www.wiley.com.

Library of Congress Cataloging-in-Publication Data:

ISBN 9781119597735 (Hardcover)

ISBN 9781119597773 (ePDF)

ISBN 9781119597759 (ePub)

Cover photograph: © Steve Bonini

Cover design: Paul McCarthy

Printed in the United States of America

V10017690_022120

To Betsy Bulleit, since this was her idea

"It was never just a question of escape.
It was also a question of transformation."

Michael Chabon
The Amazing Adventures of Kavalier & Clay

"The city gave its name to the power of patience—Romanita. Romanita excludes emotion, hurry, doubt. Romanita waits, sees the moment and moves ruthlessly when the time is right. Romanita rests on an absolute conviction of ultimate success and arises from a single principle, Cunctando regitur mundus: *waiting, one conquers all.*"

Mary Doria Russell
The Sparrow

"How much more of life we live than we remember."

John Le Carré
The Secret Pilgrim

Contents

Be Proactive
(Problems Do Not Resolve Themselves)

One Sip

STANDING REGALLY ON STAGE, Deirdre Mahlan, president of Diageo North America, leans into the microphone and says to the audience, "Join me in welcoming the founder of the Bulleit brand ... *Tom Bulleit.*"

The roar from the crowd thunders as I jog up the steps to the stage and hug Deidre, who is applauding now, a grin spread across her face. I arrive at the podium and look out at the hundreds of invited guests packed inside this tent the size of a big top. A kaleidoscope of faces whirls before me—dozens of Diageo folks, members of the media, local and state politicians, my family, and scores of friends, some who've traveled thousands of miles to celebrate this day, this momentous event.

Suddenly, I feel weak-kneed and disoriented, barraged by emotions—joy, gratitude, humility, validation, even *shock*.

And love. I feel enormous love.

The applause soars, peaks, ebbs, and then silence descends, humming with expectation, the only sound the thumping of the wind against the canvas of the tent. I pause to catch my breath.

1

I peer at the crowd, these hundreds of people eyeing me, waiting, many beaming, some leaning forward on their folding chairs, some holding their programs wound tight in their fists, the wind outside continuing to sing.

I smile and extend my left hand like a game show host pointing out the grand prize. We are on the grounds of the first Bulleit Bourbon distillery, occupying 300 acres of rolling Kentucky countryside. On this campus, we've built four of what will eventually be 12 barrel houses, each holding 55,000 barrels of bourbon, and a 52-foot still—the land, the construction, irrigation system, solar panels, the whole works coming in at a cost somewhere north of $250 million. In a few minutes, along with Deirdre, the governor of Kentucky, one of the senators from our state, and a few other dignitaries, I will wield a pair of ridiculously oversized shears and cut the ribbon dedicating the distillery. But now, I shake my head in wonder.

"I was sitting in the audience," I say, my hand frozen in mid-gesture, "and I was thinking if all this could happen, I should buy a lottery ticket, because I could win the lottery."

I lower my head to a ripple of laughter. I smooth my tie, and say, "Thank you all for coming. This is an extraordinary day. I thought, mistakenly, that this would be a day like many others. I don't know what I was thinking. Sometimes I can speak well, but today—"

I can't hold the emotion back. I clear my throat, grip the podium with both hands, and say, "I hope you will forgive me. Today I'm a little bit overwhelmed by my wedding anniversary."

Another laugh, followed by another surge of applause.

"Thirty years," I say. "Betsy and I. *Thirty years.* That's when we officially started our journey together. And that's when all this began. Of course, if I go back to the very beginning, when my great-great-grandfather Augustus created the original recipe for Bulleit Bourbon, we go back 160 years or so. And speaking of old, did I mention that today is my birthday?"

Now a cheer. I shake my head slowly and whisper, "Extraordinary."

I pause again, look over the crowd, and close my eyes. In my mind's eye I see bottles of Bulleit Bourbon and Bulleit Rye lined up on a shelf, the bottles draped with double gold medals from the San Francisco World Spirits Competition and other international competitions, not just once, but year after year ... extraordinary ...

How did this happen? How did I get here?
It was simple, really, but not easy. Not close to easy.
I went one bartender, one handshake, one sip at a time.

*   *   *

Eleven years ago.

"Try it," I say.

The brute of a bartender wearing a lumberjack's shirt and a bushy, flame-colored beard swipes a rag across the bar. He's a human mountain, six-five, 250 pounds, a three-way hyphenate—manager, barkeep, bouncer—slinging shots, beers, and hardly ever mixing cocktails in this, call it, rustic bar in Kansas City. Bars like these on the East and West Coasts have started to become trendy, some heading toward hipster, and a few places have seen the emergence of a cocktail culture. No sign of that here. I would call this a hillbilly bar, without a shred of disrespect. I myself am a born and bred Kentuckian and proud of it.

The place smells of pine disinfectant, grilled burgers, and onions—and whiskey. An American pub, catering to business types on the move or on the make sitting shoulder to shoulder with blue-collar regulars in this home away from home, or pit stop, or a place to forget, fortify, or escape. A familiar place.

I've been here before. Or have I? I've been to similar bars for days and I'll continue tomorrow. If I don't come here, I'll bring my sample bottles to another bar, and then another … and another …

I don't stop.

I can't.

I can't *be* stopped.

It's 11:50 in the morning, 10 minutes before the bartender unlocks the front door and ushers in the day-trippers. Plenty of time. I tap-tap-tap the lip of the bottle of bourbon I've placed on the bar. I grin at it. I do. I *grin* because I know the honey-colored liquor inside intimately and I know the convoluted, improbable—no, *impossible* journey—that brought the bottle and me here. It's 2006, and at this moment I don't know how the tale ends. I do know three things. One—the saga comes with some history, beginning 160 years ago in the Old West. Two—it's a miracle I'm standing here in this bar … a miracle I'm standing at all … a miracle I'm *alive*. And, three—our little brand brings in virtually no cash flow, we've got a miniscule marketing budget, and few people have even heard of my upstart bourbon. All that adds up to one simple, incontrovertible fact: I really need to make this sale.

"Try it," I say to the bartender again.

I nudge the bottle of bourbon another inch forward into his sightline and spin it to make sure the orange label faces him head on. He hitch-hikes his thumb at a row of liquor bottles crammed onto a shelf buckling behind him.

"I'm overstocked," he says.

"Well," I say. "Too much of anything is bad, but too much good whiskey is barely enough."

The bartender frowns. "Huh?"

"Mark Twain," I say.

"Ah." He shimmies his massive shoulders as if shaking off fleas, flips the rag over, and resumes wiping down the bar. "Got to remember that one."

"Good. Clearly, you have an appreciation for the best."

He folds the bar rag into quarters, tosses it aside, picks up the bottle of bourbon, and squints at the label. "Bull-ay?"

"Bull-*it*," I say. "Like what you fire out of a pistol."

He peers at me dubiously.

"That would be my name," I say. "Tom *Bulleit*. And you are?"

"Matt."

"Pleased to meet you, Matt." I offer my hand. Matt extends his in return and we shake. My hand disappears inside his palm, which is the size of a catcher's mitt.

"Same here, Mr. Bulleit."

"Please. Tom."

"This your brand, huh?"

"It is."

Matt nods and considers the bottle.

"Frontier Whiskey," he murmurs, reading the label, and then slowly wagging his head. "Bourbon's not really selling, Tom. Everybody's drinking vodka."

"I've heard. Repeatedly."

"Sorry," he says, sliding the bottle back to me.

I don't budge. I keep my eyes fixed on his. "Here's the thing."

I pause.

"Now that we're on a first-name basis, pretty nearly friends, I need a favor."

Now he squints at *me*. "What kind of favor?"

"One sip."

Matt leans both of his tree-limb sized forearms onto the bar. "I told you. Nobody's buying bourbon."

"That's why I'm asking for a favor. Or maybe it's a dare. One sip. For the fun of it. For research. For your edification. For future generations. For Mark Twain. Otherwise, I'll have to come back tomorrow and go through my whole schtick all over again. And neither of us wants *that*."

A sound explodes from Matt that may be a chuckle. An interminable 10 seconds ticks away. Time stops. Matt's forehead folds in two and then I realize he may in fact be *thinking*. And then movement. Time resumes. Matt shakes his head, reaches under the bar, and brings out two shot glasses.

"Join me," he says.

"Thank you," I say, and pour us each a finger's worth of bourbon. I raise my glass. "Cheers."

We clink glasses. Matt swishes the liquid in his mouth, then inhales his shot. After a moment he licks his lips like a bear at a barbecue.

"Damn," he says, sliding his shot glass toward me. I pour another finger's worth. He drinks that one faster.

"My," he says.

"So, just for research, may I interest you in a bottle for your bar?"

"Hell, no," Matt says. "I'll take two."

*   *   *

Back to Shelbyville.

March 14, 2017.

I stand on the stage in this tent on the dedication of the first Bulleit Bourbon distillery, gripping the podium in front of what feels like an infinity of faces.

I look out at them and I say, "I don't believe our lives are told in years … or months … or weeks. I believe we live our lives in moments."

I pause.

"That's what I remember most," I say, and that's what I am about to share.

The moments.

Presume Nothing

("No, This Gun
Isn't Loaded")

The Promise

I AM THE SON of two fathers, my biological father, the one I never knew but who lives in my heart and my imagination, and my father who adopted me, the one who gave me his heart, his soul, and his name. I know both to be military men, as am I. I know both to be warriors and heroes, and a hero I am not. But I, too, am a warrior, and like my warrior fathers, when I sign up for a mission, I complete it, or die trying. George Gage, my biological father, died in 1944 during his mission at Utah Beach in Normandy. The details are insignificant. His death—and the deaths of the thousands who died with him—is not.

* * *

I remember the smells.

I sit in my highchair at the kitchen table. My mother, Dorothy Bulleit, and my grandmother whom we call Nana, bake constantly—cakes, pies, cookies. As they swirl through the kitchen in a kind of dance, I summon the smell of chocolate chip cookies right out of the oven, resting on a plate just out of my reach. I am not quite two, but in February 1945, my father has gone to war and I am the man of the house.

7

One day, the doorbell rings. Two emotions, nearly running into each other, cross my mother's face. First, surprise, because she's not expecting anyone. She wipes her hands on her apron, opens the front door, and a man hands her a telegram. She closes the door and the second emotion appears. Dread. She tears open the envelope, skims it, and her pounding heart settles. The telegram informs her that her husband—my father—has been slightly injured in battle. My mother has been holding her breath, and only now allows herself to exhale. A month later, she receives a second telegram, a follow-up, informing her that the first telegram was a mistake. What she'd read was untrue. My father had been seriously wounded. That second emotion, dread, reappeared, but this time a third emotion followed—fear.

* * *

Eastern Belgium. January 1945. The Battle of the Bulge.

A five-tank patrol, part of the Timberwolf Division of General Patton's Third Army, comes upon a full Panzer Division, heavy artillery, and dozens of tanks, maybe close to 100, total. The Sherman Tank gunner has received his orders. His mission. Hold off the Panzer Division until reinforcements arrive.

Thomas Ewing Bulleit, my father, the gunner, swivels the tank's big gun and blasts into the swarm of converging German tanks. The Panzer tanks return the fire relentlessly, riddling the five American tanks from all sides, from every angle. Inside my dad's tank, the hammering of the gunfire deafens him as a torrent of bullets rips through the tank's metal skeleton like it's made of aluminum. My father, shocked, blinded, blood pouring down his face, pulls himself out of the tank, drops into two feet of snow, and crawls on the ground, away from the massacre. Advancing Allied troops pick him up and bring him to a triage station. Shortly after, the only available surgeon, a dentist, removes his right eye. He spends a year in England, recovering, fighting infections. Finally, he returns home, and after undergoing several operations to reconstruct his face, my dad gives up his career in banking and takes a job as a purchasing agent for Delmonico Foods. Despite horrific migraine headaches from shrapnel lodged in his brain, he never misses a day of work and I never once hear him complain. The Panzer Division assault on his five-tank patrol lasts less than five minutes, but we prevail in the Battle of the Bulge and win the war. My father—soldier, warrior—has completed his mission.

* * *

Lessons taught without words.

As I grow out of my youth and enter my teens, a new relationship with my father forms. He's no longer my playground chaperone, my bike rider teacher, my evening reader. We remain fishing buddies, though more and more infrequently, the silences between us becoming longer and increasingly acute. I drift into friendships with kids cooler than my parents—all kids are cooler than everyone's parents—and I discover girls. At home, although something about us has changed, I remain aware of my father as this omniscient, godlike figure, a tall, dapper, well-dressed man in button-down shirts and slacks, never in jeans—even when fishing—a cigarette dangling from the fingers of one hand, a bottle of beer or a glass of bourbon cupped in the other. He's a quiet man, not unaffectionate, but not what I would call warm. He is, in the best sense, a survivor, of war, of business, of life. At times—too many times—he enters the one bathroom in our house, locks the door, and sighs heavily, the smoke from his cigarette slithering up from the narrow opening between bathroom door and hallway floor. I know he's closed himself off to try to stifle the debilitating agony of his nearly constant migraines. I can't imagine that smoking helps his condition, but I tell myself that maybe it somehow lessens his pain. In the mornings, he emerges from the bathroom, sits down for breakfast at 7:00, and leaves in time to make it to work by 8:00. I don't realize then that I assimilate key life lessons from my father's simple, consistent behavior. Accept the hand life deals you. Don't complain. Don't feel sorry for yourself. Work. Keep moving forward, never stop, never quit. Work.

* * *

In 1961, I graduate from Trinity High School, enter the University of Kentucky, and major in partying. Thinking back, I don't recall a single moment in which I cracked a book or studied for an exam. My grades confirm this. Somehow—I have no idea how—I eke through freshman year and stumble into sophomore year, my dedication to partying escalating, which I never would have thought possible. I excel at Phi Delta Theta, my fraternity, which makes *Animal House* seem like a monastery. Concerned, my parents arrange for what today would be called an intervention. They first bring in Sister Aunt Jean Clare, one of my father's sisters, whom I refer to as "Top Nun," a college professor whose attempts to convince me of the value of education, fails. They then call on tough-as-nails Aunt Pearl, my father's other sister, who sits me down for a constructive conversation about my future.

"You will never amount to shit," she tells me.

I concede that she may have a point, but I do, in fact, have a plan.

*   *   *

Kentucky. Land of rolling hills, thoroughbreds, and bourbon. Kentucky is to bourbon what the Napa Valley is to wine. Actually, more so—95 percent of the world's bourbon is made in Kentucky. Later in life, I will discover that bourbon, while always in my consciousness, is also in my blood. But I know that bourbon has always been in my family.

In the mid-1800s, my great-great-grandfather, Augustus Bulleit, emigrated from Europe, landed in New Orleans, and moved north to the Louisville area. He married, sired five children, opened a tavern, and began distilling bourbon using a recipe of two-thirds corn and one-third rye. Augustus, salesman, entrepreneur, and man of mystery, would load barrels of bourbon onto his wagon and his raft, haul them to New Orleans to sell, helping to create the legend of Bourbon Street. On one of his trips from Louisville to New Orleans, Augustus and his wagon and raft full of bourbon disappeared, vanishing from the face of the earth. We've considered all the obvious explanations: Augustus was slaughtered by Indians; Augustus was robbed by bandits who murdered him, stole his money, and absconded with his bourbon: or, the most intriguing, Augustus disappeared on purpose, perhaps into the arms of another woman, a second wife he had stowed away in New Orleans. As a teenager, the legend of Augustus Bulleit, my great-great-grandfather, bourbon distiller, possible bigamist, and creator of our family bourbon recipe remains romantically etched in my mind.

*   *   *

I work summers at a distillery. The sounds, the smells, the action, the camaraderie, the world of making bourbon affects me in ways profound and small. I can't articulate this feeling to anyone yet, because I can't put my finger on it. But it feels like a cross between catching the bourbon distilling bug and falling in love. Most of all, the world of bourbon feels like my world. I see this world—bourbon distilling—as my future, my calling. In my gut, I know that I want to become not just a distiller, I want to revive Augustus's recipe. One afternoon, coming home from my job at the distillery, I find my dad at his customary position on our front porch, enjoying a bourbon and a cigarette. I decide this is the perfect opportunity to inform him of my grand plan.

I nod as I climb the stairs to the porch. I take a seat next to him. I hold for a count of three.

"I've been thinking about my future," I say.

Dad raises an eyebrow. "Oh?"

"I have a plan."

"Well, that's a relief, Tom," he says, "because your grades are, frankly, abysmal."

I smile. "Thanks, Dad."

It takes him a moment to realize I have no idea what *abysmal* means.

"What's your plan?" he says.

"I want to go into distilling and bring back Augustus's original recipe."

My father shakes his head slowly.

The head shake.

One simple movement that signifies exasperation, frustration, and disappointment without saying a single word.

"No," he says, as punctuation.

"No?" I squeak.

He takes a long sip of his drink.

"No. You will complete your undergraduate education, you will enlist in the military, and then you will go to law school and become a lawyer."

I think of our family's educational lineage, daunting to me. My grandfather attended the University of Chicago, my father, Notre Dame.

"Law school?" I say. He might as well have instructed me to land a spacecraft on Mars. "But my grades are … abysmal."

"Then you'd better get to work."

College. The military. Law school. No mention of Augustus's bourbon recipe or becoming a distiller.

But my father has spoken.

And as all fathers I know of his generation and mine, his word is law.

I don't dare face another head shake—or worse.

Without speaking, I revise my plan.

Beginning now, I'll do what my father says.

My dad and me 1943 before he shipped out to join General Patton's Third Army in France during the 2nd World War.

Be Prepared

(Embrace the Wisdom
of the Boy Scouts)

War

I CARRY WITH ME the naïve and romantic notion from books I've read and movies I've seen that I will join the military and become an officer and a gentleman. My college transcript quickly torpedoes the officer idea. A private I will be. Life, I'm learning, seems to consist of starts, stops, and, mostly, beginnings. Starting from scratch.

I'm not sure which branch of the military I should join, but the Navy seems promising, or at least the safest and least stressful. One day, in 1966, as senior year at the University of Kentucky comes to an end, I sit across from a stone-faced Navy recruiter who pores over pages of forms that he's told me I will momentarily sign. He's wearing a uniform and appears to be an officer, but based on his gruff demeanor, I don't figure him for a gentleman. He grunts, does his own head shake—never a good sign—and then laughs, hard, jarring me. I realize then that he's looking at my transcript. He shakes his head again and sifts through a few other forms.

"Looking to fit you into the right slot," he says, after yet *another* head shake. "Your grades are—"

"Abysmal," I say, helpfully.

It's only a matter of time before I will learn the meaning of that word.

"Correct," he says, scowling at the form. "You want to be an electrician?"

"I'm not good with wiring or that sort of thing. I majored in English."

"We speak English. What about a boatswain's mate? You want to be a boatswain's mate?"

"Uh, okay, maybe, I'm not quite sure what that—"

"You do basically everything. Rigging, deck maintenance, really any-thing that's required to run a ship."

"I've never been on a ship," I admit. "I've been on a boat. A small boat. Done some fishing. We have this little river—"

"How about a medic?"

"A medic—"

"Yeah. A corpsman. You work in the hospital."

I perk up. "With nurses?"

"Yes. Nurses."

I picture our frat parties on campus. Nurses, coeds, partying, the Navy. I've clearly chosen the right branch of the military.

"I'll do that," I say. "I'll be a medic. That's great."

He pushes the forms over to me and I sign them with a flourish. Only after I attach my signature do I see at the top of one of the forms that I will be heading to basic training—in the *Marines*.

"Excuse me, I thought I was joining the Navy—"

"You are. Marines are part of the Navy." He leans forward, his eyes cold and dark, and he snarls, "That would be—excuse me, *sir*."

* * *

I complete boot camp at Great Lakes Naval Installation, a virtual city of more than 1,000 buildings spread over more than 1,000 acres north of Chicago. After that I head to Camp Lejeune in North Carolina, where I train to become a corpsman field medic (FMF), then complete my medical training at a military hospital in Portsmouth, Virginia. Looking back, this timeframe flickers and then unnerves me. I feel as if I'm caught in a vortex of events whirling around me, out of my grasp, barely in my sightline, including one event that I hazily envision but appears off to the side, nearly eluding my memory altogether. Nothing that significant. Only my wedding.

In 1967, I marry Stephanie Patrick, a high-spirited Kentuckian who keeps me laughing and on my toes. Though Stephanie doesn't attend UK, we meet at a fraternity party. One thing leads to another, we start dating, we get engaged, and one Sunday I see myself standing next to her at St. Francis of Rome Church in Louisville, murmuring marriage vows to each other before God, a clergyman, and a tiny cluster of family and friends.

I must believe that I never want the party better known as college to end and, by marrying Stephanie, I'll simply keep it going. But early in our marriage, I receive sobering news. The Navy mails me my orders. I will be joining the First Marine Division in Vietnam.

Two nights before I leave for Vietnam, I say goodbye to my family. The family convenes in the kitchen for what feels like a last supper. We don't talk much, the conversation sporadic and strained. Afterward, I spend some time with my sister, Mary Jo. We say an awkward goodbye and then she wraps her arms around me in a long, tearful hug. I go into the kitchen and find my mother drying some dishes, an absent look on her face. I've always felt close to her, comfortable talking with her, struck by her beauty, disarmed by her easy laugh, open to her sensible advice. We hug and she goes off to bed. A wave of emptiness shudders through me. I allow it to pass, take a deep breath, and seek out my father.

Bourbon in one hand, cigarette in the other, he sits in his chair in the living room—every dad has a chair—and I sit on the couch next to him. The silence in the room presses into me. I hadn't expected lively conversation with my father before I left for Vietnam, but I hadn't been prepared for such—quiet. The quiet unnerves me. Maybe I expected words of wisdom from my warrior father, but I receive none. Time flicks by and I begin to fidget.

"Well," I say, starting to stand.

"Write your mother," my father says.

I sit back down at the edge of the couch. My father looks past me, his face obscured in a cloud of cigarette smoke. I wonder if he's seeing something far away, something from his past, his war.

"Write your mother and tell her you are in no danger," he says. And then he pulls something out of his shirt pocket.

"Take this."

He hands me his St. Christopher medal and neck chain.

I stare at it, speechless.

My father takes a drag from his cigarette.

"It worked pretty good for me," he says.

I murmur thanks. We don't hug. We don't have to.

Two days later, before dawn, I leave.

*   *   *

Who are you? Why are you here?

We land in Da Nang at night, a group of us, mixed up and mismatched, none of us in the same unit. We've come to replace those who have gone home, gotten hurt, or gotten killed. We have no assignment, yet. We await our orders, our destination, our destiny.

We fly commercial, served by merry flight attendants, until we begin our descent, when the flight attendants lie down on the floor and cover their heads. I blink at them, confused. Someone explains that the enemy typically lobs rockets and mortars at arriving airliners. We land then, the plane bouncing, thumping, grinding to a stop, and loud voices usher us off the aircraft. We step over and around the flight attendants on the floor.

Lugging my duffel, I walk onto the landing strip. I have no idea where I should go. A staff sergeant materializes and asks to see my papers. A few of us from the flight cluster around him and he nods at our paperwork, directing each of us with his thumb, like a hitchhiker, "You, go there. You, over there."

He stares at my papers, murmurs, "Doc."

"Yes, sir."

"Go to the hospital. You know where that is?"

"No, sir."

He points vaguely toward a shadowy hut in the distance. "Up there. They'll tell you what to do."

I hustle over to the hut, find a M*A*S*H unit, busy, frantic, overwhelmed, chaotic. I stand aside, bide my time, wait for a break in the action. I walk to a gunnery sergeant, who sighs heavily as I approach.

"Excuse me, sir, staff sergeant told me to see you, sir."

He grunts. He looks exhausted, his face grimy and lined. He wears the wizened expression of a much older man. He looks me over, then asks, "Are you coming or going, son?"

I wait to answer his question, which seems both philosophical and a golden opportunity. I don't have the sense or presence of mind to tell him I'm leaving, on my way out, so I mutter the truth, "I just arrived, sir."

The gunny grunts, gestures to another hut nearby. "Go over there, take a shower, grab some chow, come see me tomorrow."

He turns away. I stand stuck to my spot, holding for 30 seconds before I can move. I trudge toward the second hut, seeing no one, not a soul. The landscape I've trod though is barren, dark, the air heavy and smoky. I feel as if I'm in a science fiction movie, the lone inhabitant of barren, unknown planet. Suddenly, I feel a kick of loneliness so sharp I lose my breath. I gather myself, walk into the building, slowly undress, shower, rustle up something to eat in the chow area, all by myself, so alone my shadow abandons me.

I spend the next three days in this way, alone, periodically asking the gunnery sergeant where I should go. At last, he tells me to report to headquarters, found in a vague location somewhere in the dark behind us, over a hill five miles away. I march to a road where after a few minutes, a supply truck rumbles to a stop, picks me up, and brings me to a cluster of buildings, my ultimate destination. At headquarters, the sergeant in charge studies me, shakes his head slowly, and asks, "Who are you? Why are you here?"

The Heart of Darkness, I want to say. And I'm not sure who I am anymore.

I quickly identify myself, at least for the next year. I am Doc Bulleit, corpsman. I'll run sickbays and patrols and do the best I can.

As duties go, I can't complain. Or I won't.

* * *

I'm surprised, at first, by the fog, by the heavy, sauna-like heat that crushes my skin like a weight, and by the thick squadrons of mosquitoes that swarm every night and into the morning. I'm also surprised by the country's beauty, green hills rising out of the mist and rice paddies dotted several hundred feet below, the South China Sea glimmering blue in the distance. Mostly, I'm surprised by the camaraderie, the familiar, comfortable feeling of guys hanging out together, almost as if we've relocated Phi Delta frat house to the northern perimeter of Da Nang. I'm lonely sometimes, confused often, bored some, but mainly happy—yes, *happy*—to be in this company of good men. We laugh more than I would have thought and more than I would have imagined, and when we watch the Viet Cong launch rockets at us from the other side of the mountain and see them splash harmlessly into the rice paddies, we not only laugh, we sing "Fortunate Son" by Creedence Clearwater Revival, and "Light My Fire" by The Doors, and we dance.

Then things change.

*   *   *

Guided by moonlight, we move. I march, then crouch in our company of Marines, hugging both sides of the road, edging toward the Haiphong Pass. Our assignment: take back the bunker at the top of the pass previously held by us, recently overrun and seized by the Viet Cong. In a nighttime ambush, the Viet Cong slaughtered seven Marines.

As we approach the bunker, rocket fire explodes, blazing blue. The distant thunder of big guns blast, rocking the ground, then the *clack, clack, clack, clack* of AK47s screeches overhead, behind us, on both sides of us. Voices ring out in the dark. Cries. Grunts. Hollers. Four men in front of me, a soldier topples. I drop down next to him, identify a clean entry and exit wound in his forearm. I apply battle dressing, tag his hand, turn him around, send him back, alive, prayerful. He hasn't dodged a bullet. But he has dodged *the* bullet. The mortal bullet.

We arrive at the base of Haiphong Pass. Three Marines lie on the ground. The first one I come to is dead. The next one groans, bloodied, his body ripped by shrapnel. He will survive, I think, unless the shrapnel has severed an artery. Then I can't save him. Above my pay grade. Above everyone's pay grade, except God's. Two Marines attend the third man down. They've cut his pants leg to his thigh and wrapped a tourniquet above his knee. I launch myself between them, search for excessive bleeding, administer morphine. He'll live, I believe. He'll live, I pray.

The sergeant's order, a subdued shout, pierces the air like a gunshot, "Up the hill, men. Squads two and four left, three and five right, squad one in the center. Doc, you're with two. Go!"

We begin the climb and a hail of grenades arches toward us. We duck, we tumble, we zigzag away from the fiery explosions, dirty smoke, kicked-up dirt, the dull light. Then—screaming, shouting, and I find three men from squad three heaped in a crevice on the hill. Two lift each other up, stand unsteadily, their backs swaying, their bodies weaving, and descend the hill. I grab the third Marine, squat, sling him over my back, and carry him down, following the others. At the bottom of the hill, I hand him off to an awaiting circle of Marines, then turn and crabwalk back uphill, clinging to a low wall of spiked brush, pulling myself upward. Above me, mortar rounds and tracers light up the night. Battered moonlight, I think, and then I see shadows dancing, darting, flailing, or … wait … I *believe* I see them. I don't know. But then I come to more men on the ground, wounded, some able to walk, others I fear may never walk again. The walking wounded help their fallen brothers. I sift through bodies. I come to the dead. I leave them. I have to. I have no other choice.

The smoke from gunfire and mortar fire rolls in, thick as fog. Machine gun fire cracks all around me, a brutal drumbeat, a blistering soundtrack. I help another wounded man down the hill, panting as I go, my body aching, my back straining. I turn to make the climb again, catch two wounded soldiers hobbling from the dark side of the hill.

"It's easier up the backside, Doc," one says, pointing in that direction.

I go that way, and do find the climb easier. At the top, I see a crowd, a melee, slithery figures running, tripping, falling, taking cover, firing. Then something whizzes by my ear. A bullet. Then another bullet screams, and another, then the air rains bullets, storms of dust and sand ripping around me, biting my legs, my side, my hands. I bend to peer into the distance and decide I may be caught in a crossfire, Company C firing into the bunker, at the Viet Cong, with us in the way. I turn from the front side, roll back, rise, and head back down to the bottom of the hill. Moving slowly, I drip sweat and smell blood, not my own, I determine. Then—pulsating flashes of light, of fire, of swirling black smoke, and then, unmistakably, the smell of death. Behind me, squads two and three lob grenades into the bunker, blasting out the Viet Cong. I keep inching downhill, tasting gunpowder, the odor of death seeping through my clothes.

The brilliant colors fade out and then—nothing. A gray pallor. Silence. In a heartbeat, the horror movie I've wandered into ends. I head toward camp, feeling dazed, tripping over shadows, the taste of gunpowder still caked in my mouth, the stench of death oozing out of my skin.

I come to bodies. I stop at each one, praying the dead I see are not dead. I check for a pulse, an eye blink, a whisper of breath. I pore over the dead, searching for the living.

Kneeling by a body, I reach for a pulse and my fingers sink to the bone, the Marine's hand attached by only a frayed ligament. I search for further wounds and find a tiny, bloodless hole in his abdomen. I fall back, sit on the road, squint up at the sky. Lifeless. I close my eyes and picture the word, the letters—*Life. Less.* Less than life? What does that mean? What the hell does that *mean?*

We're all dead, I think. Us. Them. All of us. The odor of death burning my nostrils, I look back at the dead Marine before me and I think, *why?*

What brings men to this?

*   *   *

Sometime later, the weeks melding into months, I corner my gunnery sergeant.

"Gunny," I say, "I'm requesting a day off."

He glares at me. Apparently, no one has ever before asked him for a day off.

"What?" he says.

"I need to go to Da Nang."

"What for?"

"I want to take the LSAT."

"The LS-*what?*"

"The LSAT. The exam to get into law school."

"What the hell."

"I know," I say. I consider telling him about the promise I made to my father, look at his scowling face, think better of it.

"They give this test in Da Nang?" he says.

"Takes pretty much all day," I say, then I laugh. "Law school, right?"

"What the *hell,*" Gunny says again, meaning *no,* moving away from me.

I wait him out. A few weeks later, I approach him after he's downed several beers with his buddies at the NCO club.

"Sorry, to bother you, Gunny, but I was wondering about taking the LSAT? In Da Nang? Remember I told you about it—"

"The LSA *Tee* for *law* school," Gunny says. "I remember."

He starts to teeter, catches himself. He stares at me. He shows no recognition. He scrutinizes my face, trying to place me.

"Da Nang, right?" he says finally.

"Yes, sir. It's actually in a few days—"

Gunny grunts. Calling over his shoulder, "What the hell," this time meaning *yes*.

Gunny arranges for a Jeep and a driver who's either a professional racecar driver or insane. He roars down dirt roads, accelerates onto the one asphalt road, a coastal highway, Highway 1, the Jeep fishtailing, swerving, at one point barely missing a farmer leading a yoked water buffalo. Riding shotgun, I cling to my door, occasionally glancing over my shoulder at the other member of our party, a machine gunner standing in the back of the Jeep, manning a M60 that protrudes from the back like a steel snout. Eventually, in a cloud of dust, we arrive at Da Nang, a resort town—soldiers, sailors, civilians clustered around stalls selling food, clothing, cookware, and beauty supplies. The driver parks the Jeep and I go in search of the testing site. After several failed tries, I find it, a tent not far from a string of bars. I walk in and the test administrator greets me with a knowing nod. He seems to be expecting me. He brings me to my assigned spot, a small card table. I unholster my .45 pistol, place it on the table, sit down, and begin taking the test. After completing the first page of questions, I know I will pass. I've studied the *LSAT Guide* some, preferring to lose myself in Tolstoy's *War and Peace*, but I feel in control of these questions and answers. *I'm doing well*, I think as I fly through the test. It's as though I can see my future, my destiny, my promise to my dad. It turns out I will always know how I will do on law school exams, a function not of clairvoyance, but of excessive preparation. The lesson here, is simply—*be prepared*, the Boy Scouts' wise and timeless motto.

I hand the administrator my finished test, grab my pistol, duck out of the tent, and get back in the Jeep. Weeks later, I receive the results. As I expected, I've aced the LSAT.

I now humbly offer this advice to anyone deciding to take the LSAT. Study, sleep the night before, and bring a pistol. Worked for me.

If It Doesn't Seem Right, It Probably Isn't

(Trust Your Gut)

The Start-Up

BACK IN THE WORLD.

That's what we call our return.

Few of us call it coming home.

We depart for Vietnam as one person and come back another. Many of us are unrecognizable even to ourselves.

We've changed—emotionally, spiritually, physically. We return with broken bodies, smashed spirits, shattered hearts, confused minds. We escape the battlefields of Vietnam, eluding the horror and chaos, only to land in new, unfamiliar chaos, an internal war—back in the world—a world we thought we knew.

For me, to be honest, the military worked. If you could remove the tragedy of war—of course you can't; but if you *could*—what remains is a gift. The military changed my life, for the better. I learned discipline, responsibility, and self-confidence. Some of this the military literally drills into you. I left Kentucky a married boy stumbling through life, lacking focus and any real conviction, but having made a promise. I have a goal, vowed to keep my promise, but I don't have an actual *plan*. I come back into the world a married *man* with relentless focus. I feel as if I'm walking through life with a sandstone draped around my neck, a stone of ambition. I am driven, motivated, impatient, uncertain, and scared. In other words, I have matured.

Fear drives me. I fear that I will fail to make a living, that I will struggle to find my place in the "real world," and most of all, that I will disappoint my parents, especially my father. And I fear that I won't keep my promise. That fear drives me most of all.

My parents have aged. My mother moves slower and seems quieter, her faced furrowed with lines caused by worry. It's not my going to Vietnam that has done her in, I realize. It's the waiting, the daily terror of receiving another telegram, this one about her son, about me. My father, always a recalcitrant man, appears subdued, bordering on distant. A lifetime smoker and drinker, he has become even quieter and smokes and drinks even more. This is how he dulls his pain, by chain-smoking, sipping from his shot glass or beer bottle, shutting himself off from his own terrors, his own memories.

So, motivated by fear, I enter the Louis D. Brandeis School of Law at the University of Louisville determined to fulfill the promise I made to my father. I leave nothing to chance. I absolutely attack my courses. I become a warrior in the classroom and a fiend in the library. Some nights I close the place, along with the janitor. I don't want to succeed. I want to excel. I achieved outstanding grades in high school, followed that by tanking in college, setting records for futility, except for becoming a standout at every party, now, I see, a dubious distinction. I declare myself retired from that life. Back in the world, I'm a different person. I am a law student, a married man, and I will become a lawyer.

In 1971, I finished law school near the top of my class and was named associate editor of the *Law Review*. I pass the Kentucky bar and receive a job offer with the Honors Program of the Office of Chief Counsel, Internal Revenue Service, a jaw-breaking title that means I'll be moving to Washington, D.C., as a lawyer for the IRS. My mother cries when I tell her, my father nods stoically, which I interpret as a gesture of pride, or perhaps relief. Stephanie and I pack all of our belongings into our car, I say goodbye to my parents, and we move east, settling in Reston, Virginia, a quiet suburb, about an hour and half commute from the District. Driving

from Louisville to D.C., Stephanie dozing, her head resting against the passenger-side window, a stunning revelation pulsates through my brain—
I've completed my undergraduate education.
I've served in the military.
I've become a lawyer.
I have fulfilled my promise to my father.
I'm now free to unearth Augustus's family recipe and become a distiller.
Two questions.
How?
And—
When?

* * *

I see me walking into my office in the heart of D.C. I once again wear a uniform—crisply pressed dark suit, subtle pinstripe shirt, conservative tie, short haircut, gripping my leather briefcase. I look like a *lawyer*. Hell, I could be an advertisement for a lawyer.

I represent the IRS. I represent the Establishment. I *am* the Establishment. But in a bigger newsflash, at least to me, I love it. I love the law and I love being a lawyer. An early riser, I'm always among the first to arrive in the office and almost always the last to leave. I put in long hours, not only because I have a killer commute and I want to wait until traffic subsides before I drive the 90 minutes home to Virginia, but I enjoy being there. I love to work. Work, I find, grounds me, energizes me. Plus, I like grappling with the minutia, the ambiguity, the complexity of tax law. I get lost in it. I'm not bored for a second. In fact, the law turns me on, intellectually.

But all around me, as I settle into the law, and lawyering, and embrace my role in the Establishment, I see a world that's teetering on the edge of turmoil. It's 1972 and one day in early spring, 15,000 protestors convene in Washington, not far from my office, to protest the Vietnam War, one of dozens of protests that happen weekly across the country. At year's end, police arrest five men for burglarizing the Democratic National Committee at the Watergate Hotel. Then a series of earth-shattering events practically careen into each other over a short three-year time frame from 1972 to 1975— the Supreme Court passes *Roe v. Wade*, the Watergate Hearings begin, the

House votes to impeach President Richard M. Nixon, Nixon resigns the presidency, the Vietnam War ends, *Saturday Night Live* begins.

In the midst of all this, in 1974, Stephanie gives birth to our daughter, Anne Hollister Bulleit. We call her Hollis, and I don't know if it's the era she's born into or her independent spirit, but I soon identify her as a child of strong will and opinion, and uncommon athletic ability. I'll soon recognize her gift for creativity. We connect, Hollis and I, from her first breath.

*　*　*

Shortly after Hollis arrives, I decide that one law degree isn't enough so I enroll in Georgetown Law School to earn a Masters of Law in Taxation. I continue to work fulltime, attending classes at night and on weekends. I study whenever I can find a spare half hour. I relegate sleep to the backburner, deciding it's highly overrated. I prosper academically and two years of mind-numbing very late nights and extremely early mornings, in 1976, Georgetown awards me an LL.M degree.

*　*　*

I love the law, love being a lawyer, but I'm restless, slightly homesick, and itching to be my own boss. Over what will become a year of conversation and negotiation, again driven by fear, this time the fear of the unknown, I leave the security of the Office of Chief Counsel in Washington, pack up Stephanie and Hollis, and move to Lexington, Kentucky, where with two close friends I form the law firm of Arnold, Bulleit, and Kinkead.

Time flies, a year turns into two, into three, the calendar closes out the decade, and we enter the Eighties. Our little boutique law firm expands. What I call our start-up expands from a couple of offices and a reception area, to an entire floor, to taking over the top two floors of our building. We add a dozen or so lawyers and, over time, I find myself with top billing. Each of us specializes. Shelby Kinkead, a descendant of the first governor of Kentucky, over six feet tall, a charming and elegant man, serves as our general counsel and litigator. I, less tall, yet dapper, write contracts. As a point of information, the difference between *elegant* and *dapper* is height. Shelby and I share the work—long hours—and before I know it, checks roll in, we cash them, and my fear of failing to make a living as a lawyer on my own eases. At least to a degree. I always live with a level of fear gnawing at me, driving me. Fear is my motor. The truth is, I enjoy the hell out of being a lawyer.

Yes, I *enjoy* it. While I spend a good deal of time holed up in my office either writing or reading contracts, I love interacting with my partners, our clients, and even the folks on the opposite side. Business—all business, I believe—is personal. So you might as well have fun. And we do. We interact with people, we make our business personal, we socialize, we enjoy dining together, drinking together, and, yes, we have a hell of a good time.

I remember one incident that still makes me laugh. One day, Shelby and I get a frantic phone call in the office. We're being summoned to Hazard, Kentucky—yes, *Hazard*, a real name—to have an emergency meeting with some clients, coal miners.

"Meet us at the community center on Route 15," the spokesman says, his voice tinged with anxiety.

"Why there?" I say.

"We got us a situation. Terrible. Things are escalating out of control. Guys are very angry, extremely agitated. They could get violent."

"Shelby, you've got this, don't you?" I say.

Shelby, tall and elegant, and I, less tall and moderately dapper, head over toward Hazard to the location of a series of coal tipples, stations on the side of the road which feed raw coal onto a conveyer belt moving the coal into a device that crushes the coal and pours it into a truck. A trucker—usually an individual contractor—hauls the coal up to Cincinnati to sell his payload as stoker coal. I know of dozens of tipples dotted all over Kentucky. During the coal boom, we'd often take a helicopter to visit our clients. Efficient and fast. We could cover 100 miles in no time. We hired pilots who'd flown helicopters in Vietnam, mavericks. Some might call them crazy. They'd pick us up, and even if I offered a map and directions, they'd ignore that and follow the interstate, fly right over the top of traffic, practically buzzing the cars. The pilots were aces when it came to flying a helicopter, but had no idea how to navigate the damn thing.

"There are quicker ways to go," I'd say, folding up my map.

"Yeah," the pilot would say, "but then I wouldn't know where we were."

One time, a pilot looks at me after I question his navigational choices and says, "You're a military guy. I go by I.F.R. You know what that stands for, right?"

"Instrument Flight Rules."

"Nope. I Fly Roads."

I spend way more time in helicopters practicing law than I ever did in Vietnam.

This day, because of the obvious urgency, Shelby and I have no time to locate a helicopter, so we drive to Hazard. We arrive at the community center and go into the main meeting room, which we find packed with anxious and angry coal miners.

"What's going on?" Shelby asks.

The miner we spoke to steps forward. "A couple miles down the road, at the coal tipple, a whole bunch of truckers has gathered up. They tossed about 30 tires into a pile in the middle of the road and set the pile on fire."

"Wonderful," I say.

"Now they're shooting into the tires and they're drinking."

"It gets even better," I say.

"They're not moving. Say they're staying put. Until we give them more money."

"So, what, they're on strike?" Shelby asks.

"At least," I say.

"You're our lawyers," the spokesman says. "You represent us."

Shelby and I look at each other. I grin at the spokesman.

"Well, yes," I say, "but you guys seem to have this under control."

"Listen," the spokesman says, ignoring me. "I want you all to go down there and tell those truckers we're not giving them any more damn money. Not a penny more. You go down there and tell them."

"Let me get this straight," Shelby says. "These truckers have set a pile of tires on fire, they're blocking the road, they're drinking, they're shooting into burning tires, and you want us to tell them you're not giving them any more money?"

"Yep."

"Let's go with Plan B."

I don't want to crack up in front of our agitated clients, but I can't help myself. I smother my laugh with a fake coughing fit and a fist over my mouth.

"What's Plan B?" the spokesman yells at our backs as Shelby steers me toward the door.

"Working on it," Shelby says.

Shelby devises Plan B on the way back to the office. He drops me off and goes into Federal Court, where he gets an injunction against the truckers because they are blocking the highway. Highway Patrol shows up, waves the court document, and eventually, the truckers move off the road.

I didn't put this in the Bulleit Points, but I should have.

Always have a Plan B.

Especially when Plan A involves a raging fire, firearms, and alcohol.

20/40/60

(At 20, You Worry Yourself
Sick About What People
Think of You.

At 40, You Say, "The Hell
with 'Em."

At 60, You Realize They Were
Not Thinking About You.)

My Old Soldier

I SIT IN THE far corner of Dudley's Restaurant, facing the front door so I'll be able to see her walk in. I chose this place because it's clubby, convenient, classy, and quiet. They serve excellent food and pour generous, tasty cocktails. I've heard they have a good wine list, too, but I'll take any Kentucky bourbon over even a high-end Napa red any day. Nothing against Napa or red wine. Just not my style, not my taste. I'm a whiskey drinker and remain a bourbon distiller dreamer. Yes, still carrying that with me. I've recently turned 43 and have not acted on that dream. Yet.

I crane my neck, peer through the dining room's hazy atmospheric light, making sure I haven't missed her entrance. I'm early. I'm always early. That's another of the Bulleit Points I live by, but this one I consider a command, not a suggestion. *Be on time.* Which to me means arrive at least 10 minutes early. Being late is both rude and disrespectful. Speaks volumes about a person's character. Or lack of it.

So, I'm early. Twelve minutes by my Rolex, to be exact. My Rolex is both distinctive and an extravagance, to be sure, but in my current state of mind—*confused*—and in the current state of my life—*tumultuous*—I need something I can rely on, a reminder that life can be ordered, simple,

33

and beautiful to look at, even during the most disordered, complex, and unpleasant times. Thus, my Rolex. (Thirty-two years later, I still have it, still wear it.)

I sigh, absently adjust the silverware and cloth napkins, more to occupy my hands than out of any sort of compulsive disorder that impels me to be continually arranging and rearranging things. But I do like things in their proper place, and in their correct order. And I do believe that appearance matters. Consider my choice of attire for tonight.

I have on a single-breasted grey suit from Brooks Brothers, shading more to light grey than edging toward black, the top two buttons clasped. Some may think I'm overdressed for a first date, but I would respectfully disagree. A suit equals credibility, and I've noticed that women prefer men in a suit. An observation. I've also been told that women find a man in a suit sexy. I would call that anecdotal evidence at the moment, having done no actual research in the field to back that up. I haven't been on a date since Stephanie and I became a couple 17 years ago. With our divorce order pending, the state of our union can no longer be considered a *union*, of any sort, by any stretch of the imagination.

We've separated, our marriage collapsing due to five years of escalating incompatibility and a legal pad full of other reasons, all boiling down to one—we can no longer be married to one another. At present, we remain frustratingly deadlocked over the custody of Hollis, who lives with me. Hollis turned 13 a few months ago and has shown brilliance in the class-room and superior ability as a competitive swimmer, setting state records, all while displaying the typical irreverence of a preteen. Make no mistake, I will fight for custody, normally a long shot for the dad. But I believe Hollis should live with me and I'm willing to go to court if I have to.

I take another look toward the door of the restaurant, then check my watch again, confirming I'm officially 10 minutes early, or as I say, right on time. I sigh softly and consider the rest of my outfit. A soft blue Brooks Brother's shirt, no tie. Too formal, too rigid, a turnoff. Again, that's based on hearsay, not experience. For about 10 seconds, I toyed with wearing a turtleneck, but I didn't want to look like an egghead, a folk singer, or a phony. Now, shoes. Black wingtips. Comfortable, classy, shined to a high gloss, the color a perfect contrast to the dark grey suit. Final touch. Cufflinks. I couldn't decide between the Marine Corps or the Georgetown, so I went with one of each. An uncharacteristically non-uniform approach, I admit, but for some reason, I have a feeling that the mismatched pair may bring me luck. More than midway through this decade, I'd call the Eighties a bumpy ride, personally. I could use a bit of luck. We'll see how this date goes.

Yes, date.

Feels strange even identifying this as such, but I guess that's what it is. Forty-three years old, at the end of my marriage, and I'm on a date. Or about to be. When I think about it, if I am to be brutally honest, my marriage ended long ago. We've been separated now for some time, possibly close to two years, time having a way of simply disappearing when life dissolves into turmoil. I have stayed in the marriage because of Hollis, wanting at all costs to avoid disruption, determined to keep her in the home she's known for almost her entire life, believing that children need security, stability, normalcy, even if the parents have lost that loving feeling and are flailing all around them.

I surprised myself, calling Betsy, asking her out for a drink. I was even more surprised when she accepted. Of course, we're not total strangers. Even though she's quite a bit younger than I am, we've known each other for years. We've traveled in the same social circles and actually work in the same building, she on the first floor, where she works as a stockbroker, and I upstairs, on the top two floors, in our law office, so admittedly we don't see each other that much. We have something beyond a nodding acquaintance, slightly. I'll also admit that Betsy, or Elizabeth Callaway Brooks, related to Colonel Richard Callaway, a famed frontiersman, and being a descendent of Daniel Boone, is in every sense a purebred. In other words, she's way out of my league.

I start to second-guess this whole thing. I poke around with the silverware again, realizing that I'm feeling uncharacteristically nervous. I glance at my Rolex, now registering five minutes before our designated meeting time. I begin to fidget, wondering if she will actually show up and debating whether I have enough time to duck out for a smoke.

Then a rustling at the front door, some voices, low laughter, and a kind of warm wave vibrates through the room rolling toward me. I stand up, as if launched from an ejector seat. I see Betsy searching the room, the host pointing in my direction, and I wave, dumbly, suddenly feeling a momentary sense of panic, followed by my own voice echoing inside my head, "What the hell are you doing? What made you think this was a good idea? Make a run for it."

Before I know it, someone pulls a chair out for Betsy—it might even be me, but I'm so flustered I have no memory of making that gallant a move—and Betsy and I are sitting across from each other.

"You're right on time," I say, a brilliant opening line.

She laughs. "Don't get used to that."

I laugh with her. And then we talk … and talk … and talk. We have what amounts to a four-hour drink. I don't remember much of what we talk about, but I remember the conversation being serious and intense, at times bordering on grave. At certain moments during the conversation, I feel as if I've stepped away from the table and I'm observing us, and I am appalled.

You don't sound like you, Tom, I think. *You sound so damn heavy, so serious.*

At the end of the night, with the staff at Dudley's practically putting chairs on top of each other, five minutes away from closing up and kicking us out, I invite Betsy to come over to my house the next night.

"I guess I'm inviting you out on a second date," I say.

I don't know if I can do this, Betsy thinks. *He's so serious.*

"Sure," Betsy says. "I'd love to come over."

The next night I answer the door wearing Dockers and my trusty turtleneck. Betsy arrives 15 minutes late, but when I see her, I don't care. Her smile takes my breath away.

We log another four hours, some of it with Hollis, most of it sitting across from each other at the dining room table and then moving to the couch. I don't remember any of the exact conversation, but I remember the laughs. I remember Betsy laughing so hard she has to gasp for breath, tears streaming down her cheeks. And when the night ends, we make plans to see each other again. Soon. Maybe even the next night.

I may be in love, I think. *I may actually be in love. I hope she at least likes me.*

I have to plot my course carefully, Betsy thinks. *Because I'm going to marry Tom Bulleit.*

*   *   *

Four months later, my divorce becomes final and I win custody of Hollis. To celebrate, Betsy and I plan a long weekend in Carmel, California, the first time we've gone away as a couple. One night, sitting at a table in a restaurant overlooking Pebble Beach Golf Course, Betsy reaches over and takes both my hands.

"Tom, I'm only going to have the courage to ask you this once, so listen up."

"I'm all ears."

"Will you marry me?"

"Wait." I pause for a very long time. "Did you just propose?"

She nods. She can't seem to speak. Her eyes are wide and glistening.

"Well, this is all wrong," I say.

"I know—"

"You're supposed to get down on your knees."

She laughs, loses it. And then she starts to cry.

"Damn it," I say. "I was going to ask *you*. Once again you're way ahead of me."

"So, is that a yes?"

"No. It's a YES."

I practically shout it and then I—Mr. Order, Mr. Formality, Mr. Everything in Its Proper Place—get up from the table and take Betsy into my arms, announcing to the diners in the restaurant and to the heavens above one of the most breathtaking spots on earth, that, *Yes, Elizabeth Callaway Brooks, I will marry you.* Preferably as soon as possible.

So begins the most thrilling adventure of my life.

*   *   *

We marry on my birthday, March 14, 1987. I don't mind sharing my birthday and my wedding anniversary. Makes it unique, special. Plus, it gives me a better chance in my dotage of remembering at least one of these two events.

"Better be your anniversary," Betsy says.

Not a Bulleit Point, but excellent advice—

You can forget your birthday without consequence, but you will pay big time if you forget your wedding anniversary.

As my 44th birthday—and my wedding anniversary—approaches, I find myself withdrawing from social occasions, going to bed earlier than usual, and keeping more and more to myself. I feel myself shutting down, turning inward. I'm becoming reflective. One night, sitting together in our living room, nursing after-dinner drinks, enduring an unaccustomed minute or two of silence, Betsy says, "You've been very quiet lately, Tom."

"Hm? Oh, yes, I know, it's this contract I've been dealing with today—"

"I don't mean today. You've been unusually quiet for months."

"Really?"

"Yes, Tom."

I go quiet.

"Tom."

"Huh?"

"Talk to me."

I swivel toward her, breathe in, breathe out, and then like an internal dam bursting, words, sentences, *paragraphs* come rushing out, ending with—

"I think I'm having a midlife crisis."

Betsy collapses into the couch, as if she's been shoved.

"Is it the wedding? Because we—"

"No, no, it's not the wedding, it's not you, it's me. It's my life. It's the choice I made. Betsy," I say with some urgency. "I have to act now. It's really now or never. Shit or get off the pot."

"What pot? I have no idea what you're talking about."

"Bourbon," I say. "Betsy, it takes six years to age bourbon in barrels properly. If I start now, I'll be 50 before I even know if Augustus's recipe is any good. I mean, I'm sure it is. I don't know. I'm probably crazy. But I do know this. Most people don't start all over at 50."

"Whew," Betsy says. "As long as it's only that."

"Yeah. Changing my life. That's all it is."

We both crack up. Then she snuggles into me.

"Tom, it's going to be alright."

"You sure?"

"Absolutely. I have no doubt."

Then, without realizing it, we simultaneously slug back our drinks.

*   *   *

On our honeymoon, I confirm my decision and reveal my plan, which is both half-baked and full of passion. I realize I should probably be focusing on other things on our wedding night, but I can't help myself. I know Betsy will understand. She's my partner—in everything. I knew that long before we recited our wedding vows.

"You've noticed that I haven't been as quiet lately," I say.

"Yes, thankfully."

"That's because I've gone into action. I'm going to do this. I'm going to start my distilling company. I will leave the law firm, at some point. Not right away because it'll take six years for us to have our first actual bottles to sell. So I'll step back slowly, gradually, keep my feet in the water, continue doing legal work, both for the money and because I love it. I'm going to bring back Augustus's recipe. That's definite. Again, it'll take time, and there'll be a lot of risk, financially for sure, emotionally, proba- bly, lifestyle adjustment, absolutely, and, again, I may be crazy, but it really is now or never. I know that we're talking about a severe uphill battle, or to use a baseball metaphor, we're starting out with two strikes against us. The longest of long shots. But what the hell. So, what do you think?"

"Oh, Tom," Betsy says, leaning her head into me, probably swooning from my nearly incomprehensible rambling, "that sounds *wonderful*."

*   *   *

My law partner, Shelby Kinkead, either seeing a golden business oppor- tunity or taking pity on me, signs on as a founding partner in my fledging distilling company. Meanwhile, I spend hours going over the numbers with Betsy, a world-class money manager, investment adviser, and all-around financial whiz. When it comes to business and life, I run everything by her and can't get anything past her. She is my first, best, and, often, only advisor—and remains so to this day.

We determine that to get this distilling company up and running, to partner with a functioning distillery, to put together some kind of rudi- mentary marketing and publicity strategy, to hire a barebones staff, and keep this all running for at least six years while the bourbon ages in bar- rels, will cost millions of dollars.

"I will have to take out a loan," I say.

"You know every banker in town. They all love you."

"I don't know if they love me that much."

I nod, take this in.

"I'm going to put this off, for now," I say. "I need to have a preliminary conversation next week."

"Which banker?"

"Not a banker. My father."

* * *

Shortly after my marriage, my sister and I move my father into an assisted living facility in Louisville. My mother had passed away the previous year. She was the life force in our family. With quiet efficiency punctuated often with outbursts of joy, she took care of everything, including taking care of my father. She bought the groceries, cooked the meals, did the laundry, paid the bills, planned the social calendar. When she passed, it was as if the engine that ran our home had been shut down.

Right after she died, I felt disoriented, and then I felt numb. But I wouldn't or I couldn't allow myself any public display of emotion. I forced myself not to cry. A generational response, I suspect, or perhaps it comes down to gender. I had been raised to keep my emotions inside, in check. I was allowed a measured, stoical response to difficult things. That was the male, military, and maybe even the Southern way. But one day, months after my mother's funeral, driving alone in the car, I saw myself as a child in the kitchen with her, the two of us laughing, and her loss overwhelmed me, and I began to sob. My chest heaved and the sobs came harder. I pulled over, leaned my forehead onto the steering wheel, and I cried.

I've never known a better man than my father. He taught me how to be a soldier, a fighter, and the value of *work*. Work defines you and work can save you. His words or my inference, I can't be sure. And my mother? She taught me how to talk, how to interact, and how to *be*.

* * *

My mother's passing does my father in. He appears lost without her. He doesn't seem to know what to do, where to go, or, worse, who to be. He retreats into his one-room apartment at the assisted living facility. When

I visit from Lexington, he appears diminished. It's as if his whole world has begun shrinking in front of him.

He continues to drink his beer and bourbon and smoke his cigarettes, even though the assisted living place has a strict no-smoking policy. He chain-smokes two packs a day and opens the door of his first-floor room so he can blow his cigarette smoke outside. Always vain and fastidious, he'd started to let himself go, allowing his ashtrays to pile up with mounds of white ash, unemptied, untouched. Visiting him one time, for some reason, I remember when he would take me fishing. I had no talent for fishing, and less patience. But my father had a gift. I would fish. He would catch. He would wade into a pond and pull out a six-pack of bass. I could drop a stick of dynamite into the same pond, same spot, and wouldn't pull up a single slimy catfish.

I told Dad once, "You know, you really need to exercise."

He shot me a look of sheer disbelief. "I exercise. I fish."

A fishing pole in one hand, a bottle of beer in the other, a cigarette dangling from his mouth.

He called that exercise. Several times a week.

When I visit him, we sit, talk some, and mostly stare at whatever vague blue image blankets us from the TV. Then, sometime after my conversation with Betsy, I visit him with a purpose, an agenda. Twenty-two years have passed since I'd told him I wanted to become a distiller. I had fulfilled every promise I'd made to him. I'd completed my undergraduate education. I'd served in the military. I'd gone to law school ... *twice* ... and earned two law degrees, become a lawyer. This day, I've come to tell him I have not given up on my dream.

By this point, my father has entered his dotage, although his mind remains sharp. I'm 44 years old. I don't need to ask my dad's permission to change careers. But he is my *father*. I still need his approval.

"I've done well as a lawyer," I say. "But I'm going to become a distiller of bourbon."

My father looks concerned. I can read his mind. He has often told me to follow the money. I can tell he is worried about the finances.

"You sure?" he says.

"Yes."

"Well, Tom," he says, his forehead furrowed, nodding slowly, "that's between you and your banker."

*　*　*

Fast-forward.

1989.

My father has suffered a stroke and my sister and I move him out of assisted living and into a nursing home. His condition worsens. When I visit, he stares at me without recognition, routinely moving his empty fingers to his lips as if he held a cigarette. I can't bear seeing him like this, ghoulish, a shell of himself. I finally say to my sister, "This is enough. I can't stand to see my old soldier this way. If my old soldier saw me like that, he would do *something*."

Incredibly, he had been evaluated with only 10 percent disability. I tell Mary Jo that I want him reevaluated at the Veterans Administration for a 100 percent disability.

"If we move him, it may kill him," she says.

"I can't stand to see him like this."

The move to the V.A., his war wounds, and the shrapnel still embedded in his brain do kill him.

The heartbreak I feel is physical, an aching that roars throughout my body that at times immobilizes me. I force myself to press on. As he would have.

The dream becoming a reality.

Go All In

(Without Commitment and Passion—Which Are Infectious—*It* Won't Happen)

Family Business

MY NEW BEGINNING. I'm going to become a bourbon distiller, using my great-great-grandfather Augustus's family recipe that features a larger rye component than in other bourbons. To raise funds for my start-up, I decide to go fund myself. I take out a home equity line on my house, and then I take out another loan, the two loans totaling $1M. I soon enter into a contract with Leestown Distilling Company, where I will distill my bourbon and age it in barrels. One problem. That will take a good six years, 10 for my premium batch. I need bourbon *now*. I find a solution. Ferdie Falk and Bob Baranaskas, the owners of the company, summon me to Lake Success, New York, a sleepy village on Northern Long Island. We meet offseason, so I miss the stampede of beautiful people summering, but I don't mind. I put my faith in faith, then in people, and I try to watch for signs. Symbols. I couldn't dream of a more symbolic place to launch my company than in a town called Success.

So I agree to distill at Leestown Distilling and purchase a small amount of bourbon from them straightaway, a fairly common practice. I need a name. I go with Thoroughbred, buy some generic bottles, slap on some labels with uninspired design, well, virtually no design, and distrib-ute the stuff locally. I am off and running. Well, off and stumbling.

I toy with names for my company, finally decide on KenAgra, short for Kentucky Agricultural Incorporated, since bourbon is in fact an agri-cultural product that comes from Kentucky. I'm not sure if the name is catchy or a mouthful, but I go with it.

"I won't hold you to this, Tom," Betsy says one day, "but how long do you honestly think it will take you to get the business up and running?"

I run my hand over my head. "You want a ballpark figure?"

"Yes. I like to plan. I'm all about financial projection. Call me a finan-cial planner. Says so on my business cards."

"Don't hold me to this, but I think it'll take about the same amount of time as law school."

"Three years?"

"Yeah. That sounds right. Give or take."

"*Three* years."

Betsy chews on the number like a stick of gum.

"I mean, yes, I think that's a fairly conservative timeframe."

I say this with complete honesty and alarming naiveté.

In retrospect, I did have the number *three* right. I just misplaced a zero.

It will take *thirty* years.

*　*　*

Newsflash.

$1 million doesn't go as far you think.

Every few weeks, I go through a ritual I like to call "paying the bills." This ritual carves into my home equity line like a machete slicing through a stick of butter. I find myself mentally tap dancing, stretching the funds as far as I can. And while I experience a certain level of anxiety, I mostly feel—energized. I'm on a sort of high. I've *done* it. I have started this busi-ness, this enterprise. I'm doing what I've always wanted. I never look back, I never regret. I worry, but I push myself forward. I find inspiration in my father, my old soldier, who forced himself forward with grace and without complaint, despite injuries that would have driven a lesser man to bed. And so, blessed with his spirit, I move forward even when I'm writing the bills and slicing through the equity line. I get into a kind of rhythm. I pay the electric bill. *Slice*. I pay the gas bill. *Slice*. I pay for bottles. *Slice*. I buy labels for the bottles. *Slice, slice, slice*. I'm writing, dreaming, stretching—dancing on the edge of a blade. It's crazy, but I feel a sense of purpose and accomplishment, even though I'm paying the bills with borrowed money. I'm doing this. I *am* paying the bills. Nothing has really happened—yet. But things will. Right? Absolutely.

Every few months, Betsy brings me crashing to earth.

"Tom, explain to me again how this is going to work?"

"Well, you have to age the bourbon in barrels—"

"I'm talking about the *finances*, honey," she says with a patient, comforting smile.

"Oh that. Okay. Illuminate me. I'm bracing myself."

"Being the financial person in the family, I just want to give you a number to think about. You ready?"

"And eager."

She hunches over her calculator. "One hundred seventeen."

I frown. "And that would be—?"

"How old you're going to be when you finally pay off these loans, working as a lawyer."

"Well," I say, feeling a little unsteady, "that's … daunting. But doable. I heard of a guy who lived to be 120—"

"No, wait, I'm sorry. I miscalculated."

"Thank God."

"That's how old you'll be when you pay off the *interest*."

*   *   *

I will make Kentucky straight bourbon whiskey, a definition, a designation, and a promise, strictly enforced by federal law. How does one differentiate Kentucky straight bourbon whiskey from a blended whiskey? Several parameters. Here are a few. For starters, the whiskey must be distilled in Kentucky, obviously. Then you must use a mash bill (essentially a recipe, ours being two-thirds corn, one-third rye, and some malted barley) of at least 51 percent corn grain, which has to be aged for a minimum of two years in an oak barrel. The liquid may not be distilled at higher than 160 proof. Beyond that, we can add only yeast and water. The word "straight" indicates that the whiskey contains no artificial coloring, flavoring—no artificial anything. You have to earn that Kentucky straight bourbon whiskey designation. You have to play by very rigid rules. I would have it no other way.

So, after I announce that I will be distilling my own bourbon, I wait. I have no choice. But I'm nothing if not patient. Think *Romanati*. Waiting, one conquers all. You can't do much else except wait and plan. I suppose I could stand in the warehouse, stare at the barrels, and imagine the bourbon aging inside, but that doesn't seem too exciting. Instead, I consider each step of the distilling process, from the clear liquid pouring out of the still to a bottle of bourbon sitting on a shelf.

Beginning with the life of a barrel.

We must use only new oak barrels to age our bourbon.

Each barrel holds 53 gallons. On the day the barrels arrive, we fill each one to the brim. The barrels come freshly burnt and very thirsty. The first night, in the darkness of the warehouse, the barrel guzzles three gallons of bourbon. A huge amount of loss occurs in just the first 24 hours, but we expect it. All part of the process, part of the game.

As for the storage conditions, we don't use air conditioning or any sort of automated climate control. We trust in nature. In the course of the next six years of aging, we will allow Kentucky weather to do what it must, and that means confuse us with severe temperature flux. When the temperature warms up, the air inside the warehouse expands, building pressure, which forces the bourbon in the barrel to seep into the wood. The wood has been charred, resulting in a kind of charcoal filter. That works to strip away any unpleasant flavor. Behind this charcoal filter sits a layer of caramelized sugar. Remarkably, bourbon comes out of the still a clear liquid. The barrel gives the bourbon its rich, golden brown color as well as about 60 percent of its flavor. The whiskey comingles with the wood in the barrel. Ultimately, thinking ahead seven years, the liquid will go from the color of consommé to a rich golden color and I'll taste a slightly sugary bourbon with a hint of vanilla.

Due to evaporation and active leakage, every year we expect to lose 4 to 6 percent of the bourbon inside the barrel. In summer, when you walk into the warehouse, the aroma of the bourbon that has leaked out of the barrels is so powerful it literally knocks you back. It pummels you. Your nostrils flare and your eyes water. We call the loss of bourbon in the barrel the "angel's share." We say that angels come in at night when everyone's asleep to drink their share of the bourbon. In return, the angels protect us against the warehouse catching on fire. Of course, scientists poo-poo all that and explain that the loss of bourbon in the barrels is due to evaporation. Well, sure, if you want to believe in *science*. I do value science, but I wouldn't mess with Kentucky bourbon folklore.

* * *

Now, two words about the state of bourbon in 1987.

Not good.

Bourbon reigned in the Fifties and early Sixties, king of whiskey. But since then, with the bourbon reign ousted by vodka, we've gone into a screaming nosedive in sales that's lasted at least 15 years and continues to keep hurtling downward, no end in sight. If I analyze my decision objectively, this may not have been the most opportune time to leave a successful career practicing law to begin my life's act two, distilling bourbon. As I begin this—some might say—*crazy* adventure, I find that my fellow bourbon distillers actually embrace me, to a man. They identify themselves as colleagues rather than competitors. I receive a genuine "we're all in this together" vibe. I'm not surprised. I've known these people and their families for years, have heard this refrain about the bourbon business continuously: "What's good for one of us is good for all of us." I get the sense that in good times, and especially in hard times, we root for each other and support one another. I'm reminded of a quote from the iconic Kentucky poet, novelist, and activist Wendell Berry: "Do unto those downstream as you would have those upstream do to you." Beautiful sentiment and so true. We're all deeply connected and sharing the same stream.

But even with that acceptance, more than one friend in the bourbon business has expressed concern, or issued a not-so-subtle warning, "Tom, you know, in the bourbon community, we all pull for each other, but business is terrible. You sure you want to do this?"

"It's only money," I say. "Borrowed money at that. And pride. And practicality. And logic, self-worth, self-esteem, and I could go on, I have a whole list—"

"Are you *positive* you want to do this?"

"You keep asking me that as if I might have second thoughts." And then I say with a passion that surprises me, "Yes, actually. I'm 1,000 percent positive."

Now, I have no idea how I'm going to pull it off.

But I know I will.

How?

Optimism. Sheer optimism. That's how I'm made. I simply *believe* ... in myself, in my product (someday in the future when I actually have product), and in the people around me. I just believe. And further, I'm driven—then and now. Yvonne Briese, Diageo's former vice president of North American Whiskey, once said that she has never known anyone as persistent as I. She called my gift of perseverance *maniacal*. I'm not sure she meant it as a compliment.

The bottom line: I have to do this. Not from a practical standpoint. From a practical standpoint, I should give it up. I can always retreat, go back into the law. I've had the following conversation with Shelby 100 times, always initiated, I've noticed, by Shelby.

"Bourbon is a tough business, Tom," he says. "Really hard. Especially these days."

"I know it's hard, Shelby. That's part of the challenge."

He sighs and, with nothing but good intentions, says softly, but pointedly, "Just forget this. You're a good lawyer. Do what you do best. Practice law. Forget this."

"That makes so much sense. *So* much sense."

I pause.

"But I can't quit. You know that."

He sighs. "I know. I do know."

"It's about the chase. The hunt. Like going after a deer. The chase is always on, continuous. And I won't give up until I bag that deer."

The truth is, I live by John F. Kennedy's famous words: "We choose to go to the moon not because that goal is easy, but because it's hard."

*   *   *

Now, some history. A thumbnail. As a reminder, here are those two words to describe the current state of bourbon in Kentucky in 1987.

Not good.

Why?

Several reasons, but mainly—war is the answer.

In 1917, when we entered the First World War, the government enlisted the distilleries in Kentucky to join the war effort. The distillers gave up producing bourbon and instead made medicinal alcohol (instead of antibiotics) and ethanol, which was used in manufacturing gunpowder, and is a key ingredient in fuel for motorcycles, armored cars, and other war machines. When the war ended, bam, Prohibition began, shutting down the stills across Kentucky for the next 15 years. When Prohibition finally ended in December 1933, bourbon distillers took a deep breath, realizing that premium bourbon would take a good five or six years to age, meaning we wouldn't have top-shelf bourbon again until 1939. Some distillers made one- or two-year bourbon just to have some kind of bourbon to drink and sell. The bourbon was less than mediocre and consumers didn't want to wait another four years for a properly aged bourbon, so they switched to scotch or vodka and other whiskeys that didn't need to age for that long. And then—

World War II.

The distilleries once again gave up producing bourbon and went back to manufacturing ethanol and medicinal alcohol for the war effort. In Kentucky, strangely, pharmacists could actually prescribe bourbon—for what ailment, I'm not sure. By the end of World War II, we had experienced a nearly 30-year period during which the bourbon distilleries had essentially gone dry. Bourbon as America's go-to whiskey had basically died. The drinking consumer had lost interest in bourbon. It had gone off the menu. This dry spell—this bourbon desert—lasted 20 years and then—

War. Again.

First Korea, and then Vietnam.

This time, along with war, came a risk-taker, a gambler, Lewis Rosenstiel, who founded a company called Schenley Industries that gradually accumulated a quarter of Kentucky's distilleries. When the government started dropping hints that we might enter the Korean War, Schenley began producing bourbon 24/7, hoarding the stuff, bracing for another bourbon shortage. But the Korean War lasted only three years and Rosenstiel found himself with a lot of bourbon and nobody to buy it, not to mention that he had even more bourbon aging in barrels. Rosenstiel, a brilliant and some might say ruthless guy, had miscalculated. Now up to his butt in bourbon, he hadn't considered that you had to pay a tax on bourbon after four years. They called this the bonding period. Rosenstiel realized that he was about to get crushed by the taxes he'd have to pay on all the bourbon he had stored. In a word, he faced bankruptcy.

So Rosenstiel scrambled and recruited a group of his buddies who made whiskey, and together they formed a kind of liquor lobby. They got Congress to extend the bonding period for two years, then got them to add another couple of years, and finally got them to extend it a third time to 20 years. Eventually, finally, in the Sixties, bourbon's popularity started to grow. Rosenstiel and Schenley's found a solid overseas market as well, discovering that the Japanese, especially, loved bourbon. For a time, bourbon enjoyed a resurgence. Then in the mid-Seventies and into the Eighties, the bottom dropped out. Perhaps influenced by a powerful ad campaign, consumers swarmed to vodka due to some combination of the friendly, clear look of the liquid, the subtle flavor, and the colorful cocktails bartenders concocted. Popular culture helped, too. Bond—*James Bond*—was a vodka man. He drank martinis. Vodka became ... sexy. Bourbon, a stronger, more intense, more flavorful whiskey, became forgotten.

And here we are.

1987.

Jumping into the fray, beginning my personal quest to bring bourbon, my bourbon, Augustus's bourbon, back to the people. Starting the chase.

You sure you want to do this?

Absolutely.

*   *   *

So, I wait ... and I worry ... and I keep paying the bills, blowing through the equity line like a fierce wind, as the song says, *trying to hold on to what I got* as Thoroughbred sells virtually not a lick locally, and my own bourbon ages in new oak barrels at Leestown Distilling Company. At one point, Betsy and I have one of our heart-to-hearts, evaluating my financial state, such as it is, arriving at the inevitable conclusion that I need more money. A lot more.

Especially since I inform her that I've bought out Shelby.

"He wanted out," I say, with a sigh. "I'm honestly not sure he ever wanted in."

"What did he say?"

"I believe his exact words were, 'Tom, this business is going nowhere. I want to get out.' He said it kindly. No rancor at all."

"That's Shelby," Betsy says. "Always the dapper gentleman."

"I'm dapper. He's elegant."

Betsy rolls her eyes and then says, "He wanted to support you."

"He's a good friend. But he may not be cursed with my stubbornness."

"I call it patience. And it's a blessing, not a curse."

"Remains to be seen," I say.

* * *

As I wait for my bourbon to properly age, Sazerac Company of New Orleans buys Leestown Distilling Company. I sit down with Peter Bordeaux, the president of Sazerac, and renew my contract to distill, and then we enter into an agreement to distribute the bourbon domestically. *Thank you, Peter*, I murmur silently. If I were a gambling man, I would be standing at the craps table—as would he—playing the "Come" line, betting that my number will come in before I totally crap out. Translated into English: go bust.

Three years into the world of bourbon, I assess my progress. I'm hemorrhaging money, praying mightily, quietly and aloud, continuing to practice law fulltime, not daring to give up my day job, sleeping little and fitfully, all while watching my bourbon business moving forward, glacially.

In other words, I got 'em right where I want 'em.

* * *

In the fall of 1991, my friend Ed Allen, connected to all things New York, calls me with a tip and some advice.

"Come to New York and meet a friend of a friend, a guy named John Magliocco. He went to Penn with a friend of mine. John runs Peerless Importers."

"Why?"

"He may be able to help you out."

Ed doesn't say much more. He doesn't need to. When Ed speaks in shorthand, I've learned to trust him and follow his advice. So, on a crisp fall day, wearing a suit and carrying a sample case of Thoroughbred, I fly to La Guardia, step to the curb outside the terminal, and hail a cab.

"Where to?" asks the cabdriver, a husky guy with a toothpick tucked in his mouth.

"Brooklyn. Ten Water Street."

The cabdriver's eyes widen as he looks me over, eyes the suit, the sample case, my naïve, friendly grin.

"No," he says. "You don't want to go there."

I check the address on the slip of paper in my hand. "That's it. Ten Water Street. Brooklyn."

The cabbie spits his toothpick out the window. "I'll take you. Drop you off. That'll be $12."

"I have $12," I say.

I scramble into the backseat and the cab pulls away, burning rubber. In a few minutes, we travel through Queens, and then go into Brooklyn. The landscape changes. The buildings look ricketier, the tiny lawns more like dirt patches, the people on the sidewalks, sad, or loud, shouting at the cab, and then go farther into Brooklyn and we see fewer people, the buildings become darker, burned out, abandoned, the walls covered in graffiti, concertina wire lined along empty lots. We pass a car with no wheels on the side of the road, people huddled in doorways. Finally, we arrive at a large pristine concrete building, no graffiti, no sign of humanity. I also see no sign, no windows, no door.

"Here we are," the cabbie says.

I lower my head, squint through the window. "Maybe go around the back."

The cabbie eases the cab to the back of the building, where we find a large door.

"Okay," I say, paying the cabdriver. "Any chance you can wait here for me?"

"In this neighborhood?"

"I'll double your fare."

"I ain't waiting long."

I slide out of the backseat of the cab, grab my sample case, smooth out my suit, and press a doorbell next to the door. After a moment—I imagine someone inside watching me on a video monitor—a buzzer sounds and I open the door. I enter a warehouse and after a short time, an elegant, friendly man appears.

"Tom Bulleit," I say.

"John Magliocco," he says, pumping my hand.

He leads me to his office. I tell him a little about me and then I say, "I wanted to know if you all would be interested in distributing Thoroughbred."

"Let's see what it looks like," John says.

I open the sample case, bring out the bottle. John looks it over, front back, and says, almost to himself, "Bourbon. Thoroughbred," then looking past me, says, "It's interesting. But I don't know. Maybe I can do some minis. If you can get me a couple thousand, I might be able to do something."

John holds for a moment, studies me, takes a count of 10 before speaks. "Let me ask you something. Do you have any advertising?"

"No, John, I don't have any advertising."

I almost say, "I don't have any *money*," but I restrain myself.

John hands the sample bottle of Thoroughbred back to me. "Would you be offended if I offer you some advice?"

"Not at all. I'd welcome your advice."

"Tom, brands are built on premises."

I must look confused because he leans forward and says, "Bartenders, Tom. Bartenders are the captains of our industry."

The meeting over, I head outside and find the cab waiting.

"Five more minutes and I was gone," the cabdriver says as we pull away from the concrete building.

Bartenders, I think, *they are the captains of the industry.*

First time I've ever heard that.

I never forget it.

*   *   *

In addition to birthing a bourbon company, Betsy and I decide to try to have a child. Operative word: *try*. I don't have to remind her that I'm a year shy of 50. So we try. Betsy gets pregnant twice, but sadly undergoes two miscarriages, one occurring in her fifth month, heartbreaking for us.

A few months after the second miscarriage, wondering if she wants to stop trying, I ask Betsy, "What do you want to do now? I'll do whatever you want."

"I want to keep going," she says with a quiet intensity that mirrors my own.

"Okay, you mean—"

"Throw it all at the wall. Everything. Infertility procedures, in vitro, and let's also look into adoption. Whatever clicks first, that's the way we should go."

"I'm going to add in prayer," I say.

"Amen," she says.

As we begin the initial consultations, Betsy starts asking around about adoption. She remembers some friends who adopted a daughter a year previously. They had worked with David Keene Leavitt, a third-generation Stanford adoption attorney in Los Angeles, and the process had gone surprisingly smoothly. She does further research and learns that Leavitt and his wife Aileen have assisted in thousands of adoptions. Betsy decides to give his office a call.

On the phone, Betsy and Aileen immediately hit it off. Betsy explains that because of my age, we feel a certain urgency. Aileen listens carefully and after a while says, "I always ask our birth mothers a particular question. Now I'm going to ask it of you." She pauses, and asks, "If you could imagine yourself doing one thing today, what would it be?"

Without a moment of hesitation, Betsy, an equestrian from childhood, says, "Riding a horse in a field."

Aileen registers Betsy's response with a small laugh. "I knew I felt a connection with you. David and I are both riders." Then she pauses, and says, "I think we may have a match for you."

We scramble and quickly arrange a trip to California to coincide with Hollis's break from school. Hollis, a high school senior, will attend Smith College in the fall. She's always wanted to see Northern California, one of our favorite spots on earth. That's where Betsy proposed to me. We decide to take a tour of the area's highlights, starting in San Francisco, then heading up to Napa, and finally down to Santa Cruz, Monterey, and Big Sur. Before we go, at David's request, we send him a mountain of our financial records and personal information, everything he needs for the adoption. As we gather our material, I feel staggered by the simple passage of time. Stunningly, I have entered my 20th year practicing law, am now a senior partner in our firm, and Betsy has begun her 15th year as a stockbroker, and is now a senior vice president in her firm. That amount of time results in a massive portfolio, essentially thick biographies in the form of financial statements, bank records, résumés, educational backgrounds, family histories, lifestyle summaries, birth certificates, marriage licenses, court records proving that we've never been arrested, personal references, and photographs of our family, our home, our neighborhood, our town, our country club, our relatives, our dogs.

"I look old," I say, glowering at my photograph.

"That's a selling point," Betsy says. "Emphasizes our urgency. And you don't look old. You look distinguished, successful. You look cool. You look sexy."

"I look older than shit."

"I'd say, mature—"

"Let's hire a professional photographer and get some new pictures taken. You look great. I want to hide my face behind a tree."

"You look fine. Better than fine. You look like the perfect adopter."

"I look ghoulish," I say.

Why Betsy finds this funny I can't say, but after she roars with laughter, we complete the hefty, encyclopedic story of our lives, and ship the packet off to David in L.A. I'm frankly glad that he insists on such detail. In fact, it might not be a bad idea to require thorough background information on every couple, even those trying to have a child the old-fashioned way.

And so, Betsy and I, and Hollis, a gifted artist, bringing with her pads, paper, pencils, and paints, fly to San Francisco, beginning what will become one of the longest, most exquisite, exciting, and nerve-wracking journeys of my life.

Once we've settled in San Francisco, we check in with David. He has news. He's arranged for us to meet Jackie, our birth mother, in Monterey. I hang up the phone, and a wave of anxiety surges through me. I feel excited, yes, but mainly nervous, as if I'm going for a job interview or an audition. For now, though, I distract myself as we *do* Northern California. We explore an exhibition at the San Francisco Museum of Modern Art, eat at Kuleto's in the city, take in Nob Hill, lorded over by the magnificent Grace Cathedral at the apex. I picture Steve McQueen roaring in his Ford Mustang careening up and down these hills in my movie namesake, *Bullitt*, then we cross the Golden Gate Bridge, stop in Marin, then wander through the windy roads of Napa Valley wine country, stay overnight at Auberge du Soleil, and eat at The French Laundry, one of the finest restaurants in the country. Hollis raptly observes it all, drawing on her sketchpad, and then as we loop down from Napa toward Carmel, we can't help ourselves. We know Jackie is having a boy so we toss around names.

"Thomas E. Bulleit III," I say, a proposal, not a statement, immediately catching matching frowns from Betsy riding shotgun and Hollis in the rearview mirror, sitting in the backseat. "Not after me. After my father."

"How about William O. Brooks?" Betsy says.

Now I frown.

"After *my* father," Betsy says.

"What does the O. stand for?"

"Orion."

"Good lord."

"I got it," Hollis says. "Speeding."

"Speeding Bulleit," Betsy and I say together, laughing.

"Or Silver," Hollis says.

"Love it," Betsy says.

"Or Lucky," Hollis says.

Lucky, I think. Yes, he will be one lucky kid, living in Kentucky, landing in our laps, blessed to have Betsy for his mother. I picture my father and me wading in a Kentucky creek and I vow to teach my son to fish, and someday we'll all take a trip to California. He will be, of course, a Californian, a Los Angelino. But this day, turning onto Carmel's main street, my daughter in the backseat, tongue out slightly as she sketches on her pad, I reach over to Betsy, grab her hand, and share a look with her.

Lucky Bulleit.

Not a bad name.

But he will not be as lucky as we—and all adopting parents—are.

We're truly the lucky ones.

* * *

We check into the Sundial Inn, right next to Mayor Clint Eastwood's office, dead center of town, and call Jackie, who has just entered her third trimester. We arrange to meet her at Monterey Airport.

We pick out Jackie right away. She's the only pregnant person coming off the plane. We shake hands and escort her to our car. She sits in the backseat, smiling, looking content, her hands resting on her stomach, nestling her in-utero child. We drive directly to Cannery Row, to a restaurant we've chosen, and as we go, it occurs to me that this *is* an audition—for the part of her baby's parents. We find a table in the restaurant, facing the water, and I go uncommonly quiet. After the usual preliminaries, Jackie gets right to it.

"Do you live on a horse farm?" she asks Betsy.

"No. I have had a horse most of my life," Betsy says.

"We live in the city," I say. "Betsy and her brother have a farm."

Jackie nods, turns her attention back to Betsy.

Button it, Tom, I say to myself. *She wants to audition Betsy.*

"Betsy, David said you rode," Jackie says. "I rode growing up. I haven't for a while now. I would like this boy to ride."

"We would, too," Betsy and I say together, eagerly. Too eagerly?

"I was in Pony Club and rode until I entered college," Betsy says.

"David told me all about that. He rides. So does his wife."

And then Betsy lowers her voice. "How do you feel?"

"Oh, I feel fine. I'm a natural at this."

"And the baby is due in early June?"

"Yes. I'm usually on time."

Betsy swallows, then says softly, looking toward Monterey Bay. "Tom and I want to have children, but it hasn't worked out. We have a daughter from Tom's prior marriage. She's 18. Starting college in the fall, on the East Coast." Betsy takes a breath, and says, "I have had two miscarriages. In vitro." She lowers her eyes, studies her placemat. "I guess I'm not a natural at this."

"I'm sorry. I didn't mean—"

"No, I know," Betsy says, then raising her eyes to meet Jackie's. "Tom, you know, is adopted."

"Are you?"

"Yes," I say.

Best thing that ever happened to me, I want to shout, and then it occurs to me that while being adopted is different from adopting, Jackie might actually see my adoption as a plus. Then, like a sudden rush of air blowing through the restaurant, I feel the energy in the room shift. Jackie seems to see us for the first time and I know—and I believe she knows—that we are the parents meant for her son. We offer the complete parental package— Betsy's strength and resolve, my age, determination, and so-called maturity, our commitment to faith, to education, to family, and, yes, no small thing, to embracing Jackie's and Betsy's equestrian connection. In only a few months, should we pass Jackie's scrutiny and ace the interview, we will be participating in the ultimate handoff, receiving her child from her arms, placing him into our arms and into our care, forever. I can think of nothing more profound than assuming the responsibility for a life. Jackie wants to get it right, and so, of course, do we.

And it is right. We all know it. It's more than right. It's perfect. It's necessary. Now, a given. It has to be.

After lunch, we bring Jackie back to the airport so she can catch her return flight to L.A. We don't speak of the bond between us, especially between Betsy and Jackie, but we all feel it. Betsy hands Jackie a business card and then holds Jackie lightly at her elbows. She speaks with assurance, calm, and then urgency.

"We will be in touch," Betsy says. "Here is our contact information, phone numbers, everything. I'll check in with you and you can call me anytime. And please let David know what you need. We'll take care of it. In the meantime, we're going to make a couple of open airline reservations. The moment you call and say it's time, we will be on the next plane."

Jackie nods, sniffs, smiles, and then she and Betsy hug. They cling to each other, both refusing to let go. *I'm watching the definition of family,* I think.

Driving back to the Sundial Inn to meet up with Hollis, we don't say much about the meeting with Jackie. We sit quietly in the car, easing our way up the magnificent Pacific Coast, this, what I would call God's landscape, the moments of the afternoon we've just spent still pulsing inside us both, breathtaking, beating like a heartbeat.

"I've been thinking about it," Betsy says. "Let's go with Thomas E. Bulleit the Third."

"Okay," I say, quietly. "That's fine."

I have learned, painfully, that at times like these, times that are fraught with emotion and opinion, especially Betsy's, that it's best to nod, agree, and say nothing. We men believe we exist to be our women's fixers, their problem solvers, their rescuers. What a crock. In fact, we rarely solve even the most minor problem. Women don't want us to fix anything. They can do their own fixing. They just want us to shut up and listen.

"But," Betsy says.

"But?"

"Let's call him Tucker."

"Tucker."

I nod, trying it on, liking the fit.

"After my great-grandfather, Lieutenant William Henry Tucker."

"Hm."

"What do you think?"

I reach for Betsy's hand. "I can think of no better name."

*   *   *

On June 10, 1992, at 3:20 a.m. the phone rings, causing both Betsy and me to jerk awake. Betsy frantically grabs the phone.

"Betsy, this is Jackie," Jackie says. "I'm leaving for the hospital."

"We're leaving for the airport," Betsy says.

She means that almost literally. We throw on clothes, brush our teeth, grab our bags, which have been packed and stashed for a month, and catch our plane to L.A.

We arrive at Cedars-Sinai Medical Center four hours after Jackie gives birth to our son. She's awake, tired, reflective, and smiles at us as we walk into her room.

"I didn't name him, or fill out the birth certificate," she says. "I wanted to wait so you could do all that."

We thank her, inadequately, say what will be our final goodbyes, and then go into the nursery to look at our boy. Tucker. He sleeps with his mouth slightly open in his bassinet, almost purring, tiny, helpless, all ours.

"How do we feed it?" I say.

Betsy narrows her eyes at me, trying to decide if I'm serious.

"Oh, I'm serious," I say.

Tucker stays in the hospital for two days, standard procedure, making sure everything checks out. Meanwhile the nurses give me a crash course in remedial baby care. I learn how to change Tucker, hold him, rock him to sleep, and how to prepare and feed him formula. One day, in the nursery, after changing Tucker, I hold him against my chest, cradling his tiny, precious head, and I picture Betsy and Jackie, his two mothers, embracing at the Monterey Airport, and I think—

What makes family is love. It's not blood. It's love.

On our third day in L.A., we get the go-ahead to leave the hospital. We plan to stay one last night in the City of Angels, in a hotel across the street and down the road from Cedars-Sinai, before we all fly back to our Kentucky home in the morning.

As we pack our bags, a nurse loads us up with an infant care package—a giant bag of diapers, a case of four-ounce bottles, a case of formula, a large box of baby wipes, a package of cotton balls, a jar of baby powder, and tubes of antiseptic cream. I gather all the stuff, which I cram into a bulging bag and a blue suitcase, grab our infant car seat, and whatever odds and ends we've accumulated during our four days, we dress up Tucker, and say our goodbyes. A maternity nurse arrives, pushing a wheelchair.

"We won't need that," Betsy says.

"Sorry, hospital rules," the nurse says. "All new mothers have to take a wheelchair through the lobby to the curb. Legal and insurance requirement."

"Okay then," Betsy says.

She sits in the wheelchair, I hand her Tucker, and pick up the suitcase and bag of baby stuff. The nurse spins the wheelchair around and pushes Betsy and Tucker into the elevator. I follow, straining with the bags. As soon as we arrive downstairs, at the lobby doors, Betsy hands me Tucker and hauls herself out of the wheelchair. The nurse wishes us good luck and heads off with the wheelchair. Betsy grabs the bag of baby stuff and the suitcase, I hold Tucker to my chest, and start to head outside. An indignant woman's voice stops me.

"Do you believe that?" the woman says to her companion. "That poor woman just had a baby and her husband's making her carry all the bags!"

Be Afraid

(Today May Be the Day It All Turns to Shit)

Steambath

FALLING UPHILL.

A strange, even contradictory image.

How does one fall uphill?

The idea defies gravity; the concept suggests the opposite of momentum.

But when people ask to what I attribute my success, I say that my chief talent has been my ability to fall uphill.

Something—an unseen wind at my back or a gentle, but strong and persistent invisible hand—has consistently and propitiously lifted me out of the depths of confusion, debt, and danger, literally pushed me away from death's door at least twice, and made me fall up, toward that impossible peak in the distance, embodying more than safety, symbolizing success. I have fallen far more than I've climbed.

Call it faith—and I do—or luck—I call it that, too—but here we are.

Constantly aware that my major talent is falling uphill, I rely on one other talent.

I know my limits. I am fully aware of the many things I cannot do. I embrace my shortcomings. Doing that allows me to surround myself with the absolute best people, people who excel at their talents. I also find, not surprisingly, that in almost every case, the top people are also the best people. Surround yourself with excellence and with kindness. Love what you do. Love the people you're with. Why? Hell, Why not? Allow me to share an important life rule, which I call a Bulleit Point.

Make It Personal
(We Are All in the Relationship Business)

I live by that rule. Well, that rule and a list of other Bulleit Points.

* * *

The deal I make with Sazerac includes an arrangement to distribute my Thoroughbred Bourbon in 20 states. The number seems high, recklessly ambitious, bordering on both premature and overwhelming, but what do I know about distribution? I intend to move forward, always, so I jump in. Almost immediately, I realize that I may have jumped too far, too fast. I can't get a handle on how to monitor and control distribution over that large an area. I also realize that to keep my operation going—forget about actually making any money—I'll have to spend *more* money, come up with cash that I don't have. Shortly after we return from L.A. with Tucker, I decide to trim the number of states that carry the bourbon from 20 to eight. A drastic reduction, a mere taste of the action, but at least manageable.

You know the expression "under water"? I learn what that means, literally, because I hold my breath every time that I look at our monthly sales figures. I gulp, gasp, and feel like I'm drowning. I look at the figures with dread, and then hope, thinking, *Well, sales can't get any worse*. I'm dead wrong. They actually *can*. And they do. One month I'm sure I have defined the floor. The following month I discover a subfloor. The next month I find a basement. The way we're going, next month I'll be below the basement, into the foundation.

I need a new plan, a new approach, a new idea, a new … *something*.

I decide to leave the country.

I decide to go to Japan.

The opportunity comes to me through Vince Cotton, a Toyota lawyer, and the Japanese External Trade Organization (JETRO). JETRO and I share a similar purpose—to expand trade. I fly to Tokyo armed with a sample case filled with bottles of Thoroughbred. I'm in search of a new market and, frankly, solvency. Why Japan? In addition to their extraordinary sense of the aesthetic, the Japanese are perhaps the most sophisticated whiskey drinkers in the world. Word is that they love bourbon. They long for it and they can't make their own. The only real straight Kentucky bourbon has to be made in Kentucky, and I've got samples of it right here in my suitcase.

I begin a slow trudge through the country from Tokyo, to Kyoto, to Osaka, lugging my samples like a Southern Willie Loman. Everywhere I go, the Japanese liquor elite welcome me and carefully consider the product—the plastic top, the paper label, the stock bottle, the weird name—and politely decline to make any sort of commitment, or purchase. Nobody ever says, "This packaging is perfectly dreadful," but nobody has to. The Japanese have a hundred ways of saying "No," and one of them is "Yes."

I get the message. Without ever speaking any words, the Japanese people tell me loud and clear, "To be successful in our country, you need a premium product. This is just not upscale enough." They don't quote *Wayne's World*, the comedy movie hit of the year, but I do. *It's not worthy,* I say to myself.

I come back to Kentucky and tell Betsy that I've failed. We will surely need an instant infusion of cash, another bank loan, and soon. But I assure her, I've learned a valuable lesson from the Japanese.

"We have to upgrade everything," I say.

"What does that mean?"

I sigh, then exhale deeply, suddenly feeling mentally, physically, and emotionally drained.

"We have to start over," I say.

"From ... *scratch?*"

"Yes. And so, I will."

I dig our ditch of debt even deeper. I don't ask Betsy how long it'll take to pay off these loans, but I estimate I'll be well into my 120s before I pay off the interest. But so be it. The trip to Japan energizes me, motivates me to work harder—and smarter. We need a new design. Something more contemporary, more upscale, something that looks and feels ... *better.*

I hire a marketing and design group, Meridian Communications, and Betsy's friend and sorority sister, Fran Taylor, as our account representative. We begin tossing around ideas for what the bottle and labels should look like. At one point, after several meetings that seem to be going nowhere, the hour late, the coffee cold, everyone fidgety or aggressively quiet, Fran, who's been staring at the bottle of Thoroughbred in front of her for what seems like an hour, murmurs, "Tom, we have to have a serious talk about the name."

"You don't like Thoroughbred?"

"Every single thing in Kentucky is called Thoroughbred. Thorough-bred Cleaners, Thoroughbred Office Supply, Thoroughbred Doughnuts … we need to come up with something different, something unique."

"Well, okay, I'm open. What do you suggest?"

The room goes silent.

"Your name," Fran says.

"My name?"

"Yes."

"Fran, I've heard this before and I know the argument. You've already got Jack Daniel, Johnnie Walker, Jim Beam, Jose Cuervo—"

"Exactly. So why not Tom Bulleit Bourbon?"

"I'm not going to do that," I say. "I don't want to draw that sort of attention to myself."

Then something happens. I look at the label, bland, generic, unin-spiring, and something falls over me like a shadow, a sort of looming *pres-ence*, and I see the image of my father, Thomas E. Bulleit. Maybe I feel an instinct to honor him, to immortalize him. I don't know. But at that moment, I know that giving my bourbon our name is somehow right.

"I can't do my whole name," I say to the design team. "But maybe we can call it Bulleit Bourbon. We'll keep Thoroughbred for the 100 proof, for now."

A whoosh of approval flutters through the room like a warm breeze. Or maybe I feel the design team's communal expression of relief. In any case, Fran and the rest of the team grin all at once. A team grin. Masking a silent roar. *We've done it*, I sense from the group. That evening, I run the idea by Betsy.

"Bulleit Bourbon," she says, trying it out, tasting each syllable like it's the golden liquid itself.

"What do you think? Give me your honest opinion," I say, ridicu-lously, as if Betsy would ever give me anything but.

"Game changer," she says.

*   *   *

The next four years fly. In what feels like a blip, Hollis graduates Smith College, majoring in art, minoring in women's studies, twice being named an All-American swimmer, and Tucker goes from infant to toddler and enters kindergarten. Betsy's star continues to rise at Hilliard Lyons, the largest financial institution in Kentucky, and I commute from my law office in Lexington to my distilling office in Frankfort, while slowly sinking up to my neck in a quicksand pit of debt.

Meanwhile, after frantic steps forward, screeching impasses, and late nights, Meridian comes up with a label that speaks to me.

The first thing that hits me is my name.

Bulleit.

Screaming off the white background.

Or more accurately—*bulleit*.

"It's so … *loud*," I say to Fran.

"What is?"

"My name."

"That's why we went with lowercase."

I study the packaging, the white label dressing the front of the bottle, snug up to the neck and new cork, consider it for a long time.

"It does feel contemporary," I say finally. "Even more importantly, it feels classy."

Fran beams. "That's what we thought. That's what we were going for anyway."

I look up at her. "I like it. No, I *really* like it. I even think the Japanese will like it."

"Let me show you the 100 proof, the Bulleit Thoroughbred," Fran says, and replaces the first bottle with a second. Above *bulleit* on this white label appears the swirling outline of a horse. Subtle, classy, cool.

"Really nice," I say.

"There's more. We're putting Bulleit Thoroughbred into a custom box."

"Oh, I love that. I love the presentation." I nod, and then I say softly, practically to myself, "Engineered bourbon."

* * *

I don't recall a formal tasting in 1994 with the first batch of Bulleit Bourbon. I remember feeling a sense of pride—and extraordinary relief—when we fill the first bottles. I remember loving it all—the taste, the deep, golden hue of the bourbon, the shape of the bottle, the label, the presentation, and mostly, the accomplishment.

We've done it, I think.

It being surviving the six years from realizing my insane notion of starting a bourbon distilling company to having bottles of my own bourbon.

After several sips of both the 90 proof and 100 proof, I do know this. *You can't make a better bourbon.*

I believe that with every ounce of my being.

Now, if I can only convince people to taste it, I know they'll like it, and then … *buy* it.

But to buy it, they have to find it.

*   *   *

"We need to have a heart-to-heart."

Betsy peers at me over the top of the newspaper she's reading, and says, "About?"

"Money," I say. "Or the lack thereof. More specifically, I don't have any and I need a lot."

"Define a lot."

"A *real* lot." I pause. "I'm thinking of hiring Charlie Mihalik to draft a private offering to raise funds for advertising and marketing. I'm told he's the best securities lawyer in town."

"He is. And you want to go to Hilliard Lyons?"

"What do you think?"

"I think it's a good idea."

"Say no if you think I'm out of line. Conflict of interest, anything like that."

"You know I would."

"I do know that."

"Seriously, how much?" Betsy says.

"I'm thinking seven million."

She nods, solemnly. "Go for eight."

"Okay." I pause. "You sure I'm not out of line?"

Betsy snaps the newspaper and pulls it in front of her face. "Let's talk to some people. Get a read."

* * *

As usual—no, as always—I jump in, both feet. Betsy makes a few introductions with investment bankers at her firm, they greet me and the idea of a private offering with strong enthusiasm, I hire Charlie, and we begin the process of raising millions of dollars from a corps of sellers through Hilliard Lyons. Before we get too far—before Charlie draws up the final papers and well before we go out with the actual offering—my secretary at our law firm informs me that Jim Stuckert, the new chairman and CEO of Hilliard Lyons, wants to take me to lunch.

How about that? I think. *The head duck, and a University of Kentucky alum, by the way, wants to meet me, get to know me before he starts rounding up eight million in investments.* A smart move, and as I've heard Jim is a brilliant and wonderful guy, this gesture speaks volumes. As I've said, all business is personal. I feel honored and, frankly, a little humbled that Jim wants to sit down with me and break bread before the offering goes out.

"We can't do this," Jim says across the table from me, right after we order.

"Excuse me," I say. "I'm not sure, but I thought you said—"

"No," Jim confirms, cracking the crust of a slice of warm bread, the sound suddenly so excruciatingly loud it bangs inside my head, the unmistakable sound of a heavy door banging shut.

"Jim, I'm confused." I fidget in my chair. "I thought everyone agreed, I got calls, your people were so enthusiastic—"

"I'm sorry, Tom. I really am. It's my fault for slamming on the brakes. I'm new, didn't get a chance to really go over this before I settled in. I know this isn't what you want to hear."

"That's certainly true. Jim, I'm not blaming anyone, but why—"

"Tom," Jim says, leaning forward, looking truly sympathetic, his eyes narrowing in concern, "what you have is a startup business. We don't get into those sorts of things."

"Startup business," I say, nodding, starting to hate the term. But I couldn't argue with the designation.

"Tom," Jim says again, even more kindly, "I know a little bit about the bourbon business. Bourbon is doing nothing now. Zero. Brown-Forman here in Louisville dominates the industry. By far. Everyone else is an also-ran."

"Well, right *now*," I say. "Jack Daniel's is a household name, of course—"

Jim flicks his hand over the table and then sighs. "*Dominates* the industry," he repeats.

I lean back in my chair, attempting to regain my bearings. "I have to say, Jim, I'm a little … surprised. Is there any chance you might reconsider, say, for a lesser offering, five million, or four—"

"We won't bring our house into this," Jim says, quieter, a *this is final* tone ringing loud and clear, stinging. "Not something we're going to do."

I nod, and inexplicably, I smile. I know myself. I will regroup, I will bounce back, I will see this as a temporary setback, and even perhaps character building. Ah, what am I saying? This is a blow. Where am I going to come up with $8 million? How am I going to keep my *startup* going?

But I lean back and simply say, "Well, Jim, thanks for your candor, and thanks for your time and consideration, and thanks for lunch—"

"Tom, you haven't eaten anything."

*   *   *

Fast forward.

A few years ago. I bump into Jim at some fancy function in Lexington, a dinner for local business folks, or a cocktail party for University of Kentucky alums, or some such well-meaning but deadly boring, small-talk festival, the details of which I no longer remember. I spy Jim near the bar, sipping a beverage, and I walk over to him. Over the years we've become good friends, but we hadn't seen each other in some time. We greet each with warm handshakes. We catch up on family, friends in common, current comings and goings and then, feeling nostalgic, I lead the conversation back to his early days at Hilliard Lyons and that fateful lunch when he turned me down, squashing my prospective $8 million private offering.

"I was devastated at the time, Jim, but I have to say, that was the best *no* I ever got."

Jim laughs. "I made your career with that *no*, didn't I?"

I just smile.

"Sometimes a no is better than a yes," I say. "That was one of those times. Hell, no offense, that was one of the best things that ever happened to me, period."

"Glad I could help," Jim says.

We clink glasses, sip, and then I say, my hand resting on his arm, "I believe I owe you lunch."

*   *   *

Back to the present.

1995.

Feeling out of time, out of luck, and out of money, I spend a few days regrouping, driving through the Kentucky countryside, thinking, reflecting; then I up my game and at both regular times and at odd times, I go to church and pray, seriously *pray*, while most evenings I tap furiously on my calculator, trying to figure out whether I've misplaced a spare seven or eight million. I come to the conclusion that if Jim won't put out a private offering through Hilliard Lyons, then I'll just have to do it myself. I grab a legal pad and start listing names of people I can personally approach to invest in my company, in fact, in *me*. PHDs, I call them. People Having Dough.

Then, in what still seems like an act of absurdity, sheer dumb luck, an act of divinity, or simple destiny, a man's hand, invisible at first, slowly rises from a billowing cloud of steam, reaches across 1,000 miles, grips me, and pulls me out of that quicksand pit—

*   *   *

"Getting good product known isn't the answer. Getting it *wanted* is the answer."

I come across this quote from Bill Bernbach, one of the founders of the legendary New York ad agency, Doyle Dane Bernbach, and one of the original *Mad Men*. I stare at it, I chew on it, I devour it. It feels like a mantra, as if Bill Bernbach had imparted that wisdom, spoken that phrase directly to me. I take that seriously. I live by that phrase. It is the key to every sale.

One day, certainly at one of my lowest points, a friend and client, Ed Allen, a lawyer in the energy business and a truly creative entrepreneur, sits in the steam room at the Metropolitan Club in New York City, just off Fifth Avenue. The club was founded in 1891 by financier J.P. Morgan as an exclusive men-only refuge for the New York elite and visiting scions and dignitaries from around the country and the world. The club allowed women to become members in 1988, and now, only a few years later, Ed strides across the marble floor of the lobby, past the Greek columns and nods at the woman at the front desk, and goes downstairs to relax in the steam room. As he sits and schvitzes in the steam, he begins a conversation with one of his buddies, Cleve Langton, a partner at Doyle Dane Bernbach. In this rather remote and intimate setting, the two men trade information, both acutely aware that information is power, often coming from casual conversation and gossip. Ed, for reasons I'll never know, begins talking about me, bourbon, and my *startup*. Ed will eventually reveal the following conversation to me in some detail, allowing me to imagine the dialogue in that steam room.

"So, my buddy Tom, he's my lawyer down in Kentucky, is getting into this bourbon thing," Ed says.

"Really," Cleve says. "Bourbon?"

"Yeah," Ed says. "He doesn't know what the hell he's doing."

Cleve laughs and says, "Well, you know, Ed, that's actually kind of interesting."

"It is?"

"Seagram wants to get back into that category. I know that for a fact. We do a lot of work with them."

"And they're interested in *bourbon*?"

"They are. They either want to buy a bourbon brand, revive one of their old ones, or start something new. They sold off all their bourbon brands. They have this idea that bourbon may be on the verge of coming back in. What is old becomes new again."

"Or once you hit bottom, you have nowhere to go but up."

"Exactly." Cleve Langton pauses and says, "This friend of yours may have just what they're looking for. If you don't mind, I'm going to run this by John."

"Be my guest."

"Who knows? Seagram may want to talk to your friend. What's his name?"

"Tom Bulleit," Ed says.

"Love the name," Cleve says.

* * *

Cleve finishes his steam, thanks Ed for the intel, and goes directly to his boss, John Bernbach, son of Bill, founder of the company. John talks with Edgar Bronfman, Jr., the CEO of Seagram Company, and then calls me. Ed has given me a heads-up so I'm expecting John's call.

"I want to talk to you about getting into business with Seagram," John says. "More accurately, Seagram wants to talk about getting into business with you."

"Well, that sounds intriguing," I say; then laughing, I say, "You make it sound almost ... promising."

"I'd like to come down to Kentucky and talk with you in person."

Now, that I don't expect.

"Does that make it sound even more promising?"

"Getting there," I say.

John wastes no time. He flies to Kentucky within the week. John is all business, and we hit it off. I give him a quick tour of the distillery in Leestown, we have a long, leisurely dinner, and then as the meal winds down, John says, "So, I want to talk next steps."

"Sounds like we're definitely approaching promising."

"You have to come to New York and sit down with Edgar. His idea. He's eager to get this going."

"What exactly does he want to get *going?*"

John looks at me incredulously. "The negotiations."

Well, of course, I think, but that realization is followed almost immediately by a shout reverberating inside my head—*the WHAT?*

A short time after, I meet with Edgar not once, but twice in his executive and family offices on the third floor in the Seagram building on Park Avenue, his walls decorated with a definitive collection of abstract expressionistic paintings, which I attempt to identify—a Pollock, a Rothko, a de Kooning? I try not to stare, but I do. The building itself, a practical exemplar of industrial art in the center of midtown Manhattan, has been designed by the legendary Dutch architect, Ludwig Mies van der Rohe. The art and architecture overwhelm me and yet make sense since the Bronfmans were billionaires before anyone knew there was such a thing. I'm taken by it all—the buzz and energy of New York, this world, and I think—

Someday, when I grow up, I'm going to live in Manhattan.

Edgar, ambitious, a devotee of popular culture, theater, music, and movies, expresses an interest to go into business with me. I'm flattered, and a little stunned.

"I admit it, bourbon's in the toilet now," he says, "but it won't be forever. Maybe won't be for long. Plus, Bulleit Bourbon. I love the name."

"That was a great idea. Not mine, by the way," I say, thinking how I'd once resisted calling the bourbon by my name, whispering a prayer of thanks that I'd been talked out of that.

"Let's keep talking," Edgar says. "If you're game, let's set up another meeting."

"I'm game," I say.

Some weeks later, I leave my second meeting with Edgar Bronfman, Jr., feeling that the Seagram Company has taken a first real step toward beginning the conversation about partnering with us. As I board the plane back to Kentucky, I take my seat, feeling once again overwhelmed by the whirling of time mixed with circumstance and my talent for falling uphill, landing miraculously on my feet. Put another way, I'm in a daze. Bourbon and I both have been exactly nowhere for years and now, out of the blue, the Seagram Company has seen me drowning, flailing, and has thrown me a rope.

I remember a line JFK used repeatedly during his campaign for president in 1960. He said, "In the Chinese language, the word *crisis* is composed of two characters, one representing *danger*, the other *opportunity*."

I will grab onto that lifeline of opportunity and cling to it despite any danger. I will hire the best lawyer I can find to represent me as I partner with the largest liquor company in the world, the largest liquor company the world has ever seen. I will happily allow myself to be wrapped into their worldwide blanket of brands. I will achieve the partnership position that *I* want and need. I will fight for that, and win that, and if not, I'll walk away. I'll have to.

I snap on my seatbelt and think—

Calm down, Tom, relax, take a deep breath. This is going to happen. But negotiations take time, several weeks, maybe even a month or two.

I'm wrong.

The negotiations take a year.

And I never let go of that rope.

"No battle was ever won by spectators."

—John Le Carré

Maniacal Patience

I MEET THE TOP brass at Seagram, among them Sam Elias, Con Constandis, Neil Gallo, and Arthur Shapiro, senior vice president of marketing. Arthur, I learn, has enormous power, influence, wisdom, and authority. He markets the whiskey, has final say on advertising—he runs the show. He wants to talk to me.

This is good.

I think.

I take a seat across from Arthur in his corner penthouse office. He smiles kindly and folds his hands on his desk, a gesture I associate with very grave or deeply troubling news about to be delivered. I have a sudden flashback of sitting across from a professor at University of Kentucky as he mutters and slaps the transcript of my abysmal grades.

"Bourbon," Arthur says.

"Yes."

"*Bulleit* Bourbon."

He pauses for what seems like forever.

"Love the name," he says.

"My father gave it to me."

He doesn't crack a smile. "It could work."

"Good," I say.

"So, Tom," Arthur says.

"Yes, Arthur?"

"What's your concept?"

I glance at the view of Manhattan below us, squint at the skyscrapers in the grid of Manhattan pressing toward the East River. Then I look back at Arthur and I nod. "My concept?"

He nods.

"Arthur," I say.

"Yes?"

"What is a concept?"

"You need to figure that out and then come back to me."

"I will, Arthur," I say.

"Keep the name," he says.

I leave the meeting with Arthur feeling confused and a little shaken. I call Betsy.

"We need a product *concept*," I tell Betsy. "Could this impact our negotiations?"

"It could," she says.

"Not the answer I was hoping for."

"Get to work on the concept, Tom."

"What *is* a concept, Betsy?"

"How should I know? I'm a stockbroker."

I get in touch with John Bernbach and ask him.

"Well, a concept," he says and pauses. "Let me get back to you."

He does, a few days later.

"What the brand's *about*," he says, his voice flush with triumph.

"You mean, how we're going to sell this thing."

"Yes. Exactly. That's exactly right."

"You have no idea, do you?"

"None at all. But I know who does."

He clicks off the phone.

*   *   *

I'm a lawyer, but to negotiate with Seagram, I *need* a lawyer. Even though I use my law degree in some form or another every waking minute of my life, I live by yet another rule, perhaps another Bulleit Point—*never represent yourself*. Having said that, I also believe that you need to do everything you can yourself. To start with, I have to be careful not to burn through a lot of capital. Or as I like to call it, money I don't have. I don't want a big staff of lawyers, a whole team of high-priced attorneys. I do want the best lawyer I can find, someone who gets what's happening. I'm only trying to protect my company, my bourbon, my brand, my name, and my financial life. That's all.

I immediately call Roger Witten, a friend from our Washington, D.C., days. Roger and another lawyer, Jim Quarles, and I lived near each other in Virginia while I worked for the government and commuted to Georgetown. We became close, and our families became close. We all had babies at the same time, within a month of one another, all born in the same maternity ward at Fairfax Hospital. When I left for Lexington, Roger moved to New York with Wilmer, Cutler, and Pickering, a prestigious law firm. I tell him the development with Seagram and tell him I need him. He comes aboard, a man after my own heart, who always goes all in.

Roger understands, as I do, that the law is a matter of diagnostics. In negotiations, you have to grasp each proposal, the text, and especially the subtext, analyze what we can get, know what the other side can give, and know what I need, and what I am willing to give up. It may seem simple. It is not.

To complicate these negotiations even more, I deal Roger a tough hand to play. To be blunt, my particular situation appears to be unique in the history of negotiations, and not in a good way. Our situation I would call, frankly, pathetic. I'm tasking Roger to negotiate a great deal for me with Seagram, that's all, nothing less. This may be tricky since, as if I've already determined, I'll never scare up any backers should the negotiations fall apart. Peering in the distance, I don't see a lot of venture capitalists standing around, panting, dying to go into business with me. So this is kind of all or nothing. And, as I may have mentioned once or twice, bourbon is in the crapper. Nobody's drinking it, fewer are buying it.

Bottom line, in any negotiation, to make a good deal, you need leverage. Somewhere, you have to find *leverage*.

I have none.

Zero.

Actually, I have minus zero.

I, Sir Startup, am going up against Seagram, the largest beverage-alcohol company the world has ever seen. David versus Goliath.

I have *no* leverage.

"You have plenty of leverage," Roger says.

As I look at him blankly, searching for the irony, finding none, he says, "You have a bourbon company, which they want; you have your name, which they love; and you have Edgar Bronfman, Jr., who wants to make a deal."

"We both want to make a deal," I say.

"My job is simply to look far into the distance, to play the long game. And while doing that, I need to create a collaborative environment."

"I get that. Both parties need to feel that we're moving forward, slowly, but steadily. The key word is progress. If not real progress, at least the illusion of progress."

Roger nods, and says, "We also have to be realistic. If I come back to you on something and say, 'I don't think they're going to agree to that,' I don't think we should press that point."

"Agreed, 100 percent," I say. "Let's put our emphasis on what we think we can *achieve*."

That, of course, is the key to any negotiation.

"Now, one more thing, the most important thing," Roger says. "Are you in a hurry?"

I take this in, and after some thought, I say, "In other words, due to my particular set of circumstances, financial stress, and so forth, do I need to make a deal *tomorrow?*"

"Exactly."

"The answer is yes."

"Okay."

"However."

He waits.

"Roger," I say. "Take your time. Take all the time you need. The other leverage you have is me. I will wait them out. I will wear them down. Nobody has more perseverance than I do."

*   *   *

John Bernbach, the quintessential businessman, meaning he knows how to *delegate*, comes through. He sets me up with a brilliant creative team headed by the M&M boys, Jack Mariucci, a magnificent artist, and his partner, Bob Mackell, a mad genius and the ultimate pitchman, both former Doyle Dane Bernbach *Mad Men*.

"Bob will create your concept and sell it to Arthur," John says.

"No pressure, but are you sure?"

"If Bob can't sell the concept, nobody can."

"Excellent," I say. "That's great."

I don't have a lot riding on selling the concept to Arthur, I think. *I only have everything.*

* * *

Bob Mackell dives in. He starts by informing me that he needs to learn everything he can about bourbon and a little bit about me. I go with educating him about bourbon first. I raid my personal library and send him a box full of my favorite books about whiskey, distilling, and Kentucky. I don't hear from Bob for weeks, he goes radio silent; but one day he calls and tells me he's read every one of the books and he's ready to come to Kentucky to learn about me.

"Observe me in my natural habitat," I say.

"That's it," Bob says.

"You sound like Margaret Mead," I say.

"I've been told there's a resemblance," Bob says.

I arrange a trip and give Bob the royal tour—Lexington and the University of Kentucky campus, historic Keeneland Race Course, a leisurely drive through the rolling Kentucky countryside, ending with a visit to the distillery. We conclude that by popping into the warehouse and taking a look at the bourbon aging in barrels.

"Fun, isn't it?" I say.

"Like watching paint dry," Bob says.

"Not quite as exciting," I say.

Bob nods, scribbles some notes.

We then head back to Lexington and sample some bourbon at Dudley's. The bartender, a friend, lines up five shot glasses and fills each one with a splash of a different bourbon. I call it a bourbon flight. Bob sips them all, tastes each one deeply, and absorbs this and everything he's seen and experienced on our tour—the bar, the bourbon, the landscape, the color, the history, the taste, the smells, the feel. All of it.

"Fascinating place," Bob says. "I get a sense of old mixed with new. Something modern combined with a hint of the Old West."

"Well said," I say.

Bob finishes the last of his bourbon flight and vaults off his barstool. Mackell played defensive end at Northwestern and speaks with the flat, All-American, good natured feel of the Midwest. I open the door as we leave the bar and step out into the Kentucky night. A bright Kentucky full moon pelts us with moonlight, and typical of Kentucky, the temperature has dropped 15 degrees in the hour since we walked into the bar.

"Cold out here," Bob says. "Reminds me of New York."

"Not in the least," I say.

He laughs, we shake hands, and I look up at him.

Yes. *Up* at him.

Bob stands six two and still carries a football player's build through his chest and shoulders. I'm thin, wiry, and top out at five seven. We must've made quite a pair walking the Lexington streets these past couple of days. I start to laugh.

"I was just thinking of the movie, *Twins*," I say.

"Arnold Schwarzenegger and Danny DeVito."

"Yep."

"That's us," Bob says.

"I'm clearly Schwarzenegger," I say.

A few weeks later, we meet back in New York. We have been summoned to the Seagram building to present our concept to the powers that be. This is it. The moment of truth. I wear a sport coat, no tie, a Brooks Brothers shirt, my Rolex, and my lucky mismatched cufflinks, the Marine Corps on one wrist, the Georgetown on the other. I'm ready. But first I call Roger to find out where we stand.

"Hypothetically," I say, "if Bob's concept bombs, where are we?"

"If Arthur doesn't buy it?"

"Yes."

"Up a Kentucky creek."

"As in, the negotiations could stall, or worse case, fall apart?"

I rub my hand over my head. Another answer I hadn't wanted to hear.

"Hypothetically," Roger says, not convincingly.

*   *   *

Bob, it turns out, has come up with two concepts he wants to pitch to me. He wants me to sign off on them before he presents to the Seagram brass. Frankly, I'd rather not hear either idea. I prefer that Bob pitch the concept to me at the same time he pitches Seagram's.

"It doesn't work that way," he says. "We can't equivocate. Looks weak. We have to go in strong. Never give people a choice—"

I finish his thought. "They inevitably pick the wrong one."

"You got it. Second, we don't pitch Arthur. Not at first. We start at the bottom, literally, and work our way up, from floor to floor, hoping for the go-ahead from each division. It's like climbing a ladder. We end *up* at Arthur. Hopefully."

"If not?"

"It not, we'll get a very polite no. It'll be something like, 'Oh, that was really, really *nice*, terrific, we'll talk about it and get back to you, oh, sorry, I have to leave for the Hamptons, thanks for coming in.' And we're dismissed. We go home."

"Can't do that," I say, low, practically under my breath. "We don't want to go home."

We begin in the bottom floor conference room at Seagram, with Bob standing at the head of the table. I hate drawing attention to myself, so I decline the offer to sit at the opposite end, at that head of the table, and instead grab a chair closest to Bob. As several buttoned-up young Seagram's execs stream in, Bob stares at them and frowns. The young people take their seats and Bob bends over and whispers, "I can tell you this, Tom. These kids have never even been in a fistfight."

I look up at him.

"Well, obviously, you have been in a few," I say.

He shrugs.

I've been in three, I think. All in high school, my Catholic boys high in Louisville. We got the word the first day of school from the principal: you cannot misbehave, but you can fight. I retired with the following record—one win, one loss, one draw. Bob, whom I will call from that moment on, a brilliant thug, greets everyone, waits for them to settle, goes into a brief introduction, and then launches into his pitch. Eyeing me, measuring my reaction, he reveals his first of two concepts. Bob keeps his voice steady, his gestures to a minimum, and goes into a concept for our bourbon that has something to do with guns, targets, shooting, bullets. Get it? Bullets. Bulleit. *Bullets*.

Right before he finishes, Bob and I make eye contact. I know he's thinking, *Well? What do you think?*

And I'm thinking—*This is awful, and silly, and … I hate it.*

"Your thoughts, Tom?" Bob says.

"What's the second concept, Bob?"

"You mean, the real one?"

That gets a laugh from the children in their matching gray suits, none of whom have ever been in a fistfight, which is what I anticipate lies ahead. A hypothetical fistfight.

"Frontier Whiskey," Bob says.

The room goes quiet.

"The word *frontier* connotes both the contemporary, as in the 'new frontier,' the idea of exploration, daring to enter uncharted territory, and the traditional, the timeless, a rugged authenticity, as in the Old West."

Augustus's recipe today, I think.

"The old and new, authentic and contemporary."

I pause. Behind me, I hear the young executives nervously shifting in their seats.

"I absolutely love it," I say.

And then Bob goes into his real pitch, the one he has rehearsed, the one he will deliver. Unlike his previous pitch, with the first concept, which he delivered in a flat, nasally semi-monotone, Bob ups his game. He *performs* this pitch. He appears as if he's putting on a one-man show on Broadway. He raises his voice at certain points, drops down to a stage whisper at others. He points, he thrusts his arms, he gestures. He doesn't pitch for long; he pitches for exactly the right amount of time. He has found a perfect length to hold our attention, to whet our appetites, to entice us with the possibilities of this new product, this Bulleit Frontier

Whiskey, something old, something new, something truly authentic, and a real glimpse into the future. He practically makes me thirsty—for my own bourbon. I inch to the edge of my seat, and when Bob delivers his final line, the last line of his performance, I, along with everyone else in the room, applaud.

Bob grins and shyly bows his head.

"So, it's okay?" he says.

Huge laugh.

"Well, it's brilliant," I say. "Bravo."

I realize I've offered up a *bravo* because I have witnessed, without question, a performance the likes of which I have never seen.

"Encore!" somebody shouts, and everyone laughs.

"Okay, now let's take this show on the road," Bob says.

We clamber out of the conference room and the swarm of young, suited, never-been-in-a-fistfight executives mob Bob, offer compliments and congratulations, and then Bob and I and one or two others take the elevator to the next floor, the next stop on our pitch tour, the next show.

For that is what it is—a show.

On the second floor, we go to another conference room and Bob pitches the Frontier Whiskey concept and, when he finishes, the person running that meeting beams and seems on the verge of applause. He offers his congratulations, his go-ahead, and leaping another metaphorical hurdle, we grab the elevator to the next floor, going up to the next tier of power in the building, and this time, in an impressively appointed corner office, Bob repeats the Frontier Whiskey pitch—word for word, gesture for gesture, inflection for inflection. Again, we're given the go-ahead, and we take the elevator to the next floor, where Bob again repeats his spiel, an exact replica of all the other Frontier Whiskey pitches he's given. An *exact* repeat performance.

As we head into yet another office for the third or fourth or fifth consecutive pitch, I find that I'm so in awe, I can't speak. Bob has replicated the exact same pitch, in precisely the same tone, using the same words, inflection, and identical gestures at the same exact time. He is some combination of a machine and a Broadway actor. I'm so taken by him that I realize I have paid absolutely no attention to the concept. I'm completely riveted by his performance. I know I'm experiencing something for the one and only time in my lifetime. I'm witnessing a classic pitchman at work, a sort of genius in action.

"We are on a roll, Tom," he says, grinning. "Top of the line." He pauses, then adds. "End of the line."

I snap out of my daze. "Arthur?"

"That's right. We're going to pitch the Frontier Whiskey concept to Arthur."

Arthur. We've made it to the top of the chain. End of the line. At this moment, the negotiations have hit pause. Arthur holds all the cards. He holds my destiny in his hands.

Bob and I walk into Arthur's office. Arthur welcomes us warmly, points us to a couple of chairs. I take one, Bob doesn't.

"If you don't mind, Arthur, I'd rather stand."

"Suit yourself," Arthur says, and takes his seat behind his desk.

"So, what do you have?" Arthur says. "What's the new concept?"

No small talk, no preliminaries, no warmup. Let's do this.

Bob begins his pitch.

If anything, he's better than he's ever been—with every word, gesture, inflection, nuance exactly the same.

When he finishes, I press my sweaty palms together, about to applaud. I stop myself. I look over at Arthur, who appears to be studying the ceiling, his hands pressed together formed into a teepee. He could be in prayer.

After a five-second hold that feels like an hour, Arthur says, simply, rolling the words of the concept over in his mind, "Frontier Whiskey."

Then he just nods.

He looks at Bob, and then turns to me. "You know, Tom, we don't field products in open molds."

Translation.

He's bought the concept and now let's move on.

"We'll have to design and build the glass," he says. "We'll have to design and build and *test* the glass." Arthur breaks apart his finger tepee and flutters his fingers over his desk as if spreading invisible confetti. "We take the concept, the glass, and we do research, focus groups, the whole thing."

I shift in my chair. "Well, who would pay for this?"

Arthur reconstructs his finger teepee. "We would."

"You're right, Arthur," I say. "Let's build the glass."

He's bought the concept. We're taking the next step. I feel it. We're in the Seagram building. For the first time in months, I can breathe.

*   *   *

Patience, I say to myself, over and over. Wouldn't call that a talent, but I would say that I have been blessed with an inordinate amount of that quality. "Romanita," as author Mary Doria Russell calls it in her sci-fi classic, *The Sparrow*—"The power of patience." I can and will *wait*. Nobody can hold out longer than I can. That quality—patience—is, I believe, the true key to any successful negotiation. But patience is more than a tactic. It comes out of my total commitment to this company. It is mine. It is me. The people who sit across the conference table from Roger, the other side, his opponents, the Seagram lawyers, just don't have the same oar in the water that I do. That are not as invested. They have been charged to make a good deal, but they also want to move on with their lives. This negotiation is not the sum and substance of their careers. It is mine. I know that the opposing attorneys have significant others, wives, husbands, lovers, families, children. They have reports to file, meetings to attend, clients to coddle, breakfasts, lunches, drinks, dinners, golf dates. They may even have a *hobby*, whatever the hell that is. Bottom line, they have other items on their very full plates. I look into the future and I see a conference room full of lawyers, myself included, sitting around a long table.

"It's seven o'clock," they'll say, pained, exhausted, worn out, worn down, several people mumbling about missing the last jitney to the Hamptons.

"I don't care if it's midnight," I'll say. "Let's keep going. I have nowhere else to be, nothing else to do. I'll stay all night."

They will, ultimately, get bored, lazy, frustrated, antsy.

I will not.

I will wait them out.

I will take as long as it takes.

I see myself as Columbo, the rumpled detective Peter Falk played on television for years. He would scratch his head, pretending to be confused, start to leave the room, stop, turn back, and say, "I'm sorry, just one more thing."

He kept coming—persistent, ruthless, relentless.

I will keep coming back, never letting up, never leaving the room.

You hear this all the time—

"Let's revisit this point later."

A common strategy lawyers use.

These lawyers then leave or change the subject, and when they do come back and revisit that point, they've moved on to something else, ignoring that first point, that original sticky point leading to this dicey impasse in the discussion. They've left that point behind, on purpose, hoping you'll forget about it.

How do you counter that?

You don't leave. You don't change the subject. You stay right on track, a bulldog with its jaws clamped onto a bone. You persist. If it takes all day, all night, all month, all year.

Perseverance.

"He won't leave," the undercurrent I hear, I imagine.

"No," I'll say, folding my hands, smiling kindly. "I'm afraid I won't. You want to know why? Because I can't."

* * *

Finally, after that seemingly endless year of negotiations, of back and forth discussion, of conversations, of compromises, of contingencies, of giving this up in order to get that, we close the deal. I'm certain Edgar never thought we would negotiate this long, but I feel both sides have won. He has his fledgling bourbon company. In turn, I receive some upfront money that I use to wipe out my debt and pull myself out of that financial quicksand pit. I put what's left into the bank, stashing enough cash to keep me solvent for at least a few years. I leave myself room to stay in the game. I want to sell the bourbon I believe in, and I set myself up with an incentive that kicks in on every case that I—or the company—moves. That's the way I want it. In the end, both Seagram and I are betting that people will rediscover bourbon. We're putting our chips on bourbon itself.

* * *

Sitting at the long table in the Seagram conference room, again wearing my lucky mismatched cufflinks, I sign the final contracts on a warm Indian summer afternoon in late September. My pen pointed at the page like a missile, my hand stops and hovers over the line on the page where I am to fill in today's date: September 30, 1997—more than a year since Ed Allen, my lawyer and friend, walked into the steam room at the Metropolitan Club and spoke with Cleve Langton, a partner at Doyle Dane Bernbach. I shake my head, picture myself falling *uphill*, once again, exhale, write in the date, and affix my signature to the last page. Momentarily stunned, I stare at my name for a slow count of five, then stand, and receive a flurry of handshakes and a round of backslaps. Sometime later, alone, I ride the elevator down to the lobby and slowly walk outside. I step onto the sidewalk in midtown Manhattan on this unseasonably hot, sticky day and I can't move. I just stand there, as if my feet are encased in cement. I feel disoriented and I feel numb. I've been waiting for this moment, *praying* for this moment—in search of validation and solvency for my company—for 10 years. Now that the moment has actually arrived and I have come to the end of this journey, I feel shockingly—nothing.

"Is this all there is?" I say to the sky.

It hits me then.

I've done it. I have made it.

Then a wave of sadness floats over me and I realize that starting a company is a chase sport, not a capture sport. The chase has ended and I feel lost. What am I supposed to do now? What do I do next? Where am I?

What do you do when your dream comes true?

Find another dream.

Be Result Oriented

(Nothing Was Built by Performing Tasks)

The New Frontier

I SOON DISCOVER, NAÏVELY AGAIN, as if I'm emerging from a fog, that partnering with Seagram will not mean instant distribution. Far from it. Even though Seagram, a giant of marketing and distribution, could press a button and put Bulleit into all 50 states, lifting our distribution from 5,000 cases to 60,000 in a blink of an eye, I get the word that will not be happening immediately. The decree comes down from Joe Tripodi, GMO. We have work to do. The bourbon will sit on the shelf until we iron out a couple of not-so-small details. First, I will have to move our distilling operation from the Sazerac facility in Leestown to Seagram's distillery in Lawrence-burg. I get that. Everything should stay in-house.

Then, thanks to Bob Mackell, my identical twin, that brilliant thug and former Big Ten defensive end, we've secured the concept—*Frontier Whiskey*—an image that I love, and with Arthur Shapiro's blessing and budget, we head into the next phase: designing the glass. Now, we just need a designer. Arthur refers me to the M&M boys for a recommendation.

"They got a guy" he says. "And I mean that literally. One guy. The only guy. Steve Sandstrom."

* * *

"Every communication with your customer should be a gift."

Steve Sandstrom

Rewind.

1978.

Eugene, Oregon.

It's come to this. Rebellion. The group of passionate, insistent students at the University of Oregon gather to protest the injustice. They feel they have no other choice. The authorities have scoffed at them, rebuked them, even laughed at them, and that only riled them up more. *They want change.* When? *Now!* The time has come. Hell, it's past time. The university has foisted this ignominy on the student population for 31 years, since 1947, since right after the War, since before they were born. They've sounded a call to arms. It's time to enter the modern era with some panache, to join the Age of Aquarius, or whatever age they're in.

Their issue?

The duck.

For 31 years the University of Oregon has embraced and flaunted the country's most ridiculous mascot—Donald Duck. Yes, that Donald Duck, the virtually inarticulate cartoon quack who in the form of some student wearing the unfortunate yet iconic costume has pranced along the sidelines at every sporting event, home and away, exhorting the Oregon faithful to fight on, *Go, team, go!*, cheer, clap, or whatever the hell he's quacking about, who the hell knows?

But recently, a rival has emerged. Donald has met his match—Mallard Drake, an articulate, sophisticated, witty, thinner duck who appears every Friday in the comic strip, "Duck Soup," in the *Oregon Daily Emerald*, the student newspaper. As Mallard's popularity grows to the status of cult following, a committee forms with the intention to replace Donald with Mallard (pronounced Mi-*lard*) as the official University of Oregon mascot. The battle begins. Another committee—a smaller one—forms to protest the protest. The anti-Mallard, pro-Donald group badmouths Mallard, calling him "sleazy," insisting that tradition matters and that Donald Duck must remain the mascot. The student government finally agrees to put replacing Donald with Mallard to a vote and the university sets a date for a student body election. In the meantime, someone decides to ask the creator of "Duck Soup," and Mallard, his opinion of the upcoming vote and brouhaha. The cartoonist, a senior, one of the editors of the paper, and someone who's grown slightly sick of drawing Mallard and has been counting on parting ways with the urbane duck after he graduates, replies with his typically wry and caustic wit, "Hey, when I go, the duck goes."

Either tradition prevails, or Mallard runs a lackluster campaign, or more likely, only the incoming gung-ho freshmen class who only knows Donald as mascot shows up to vote (back then, at the U of O, by the time you've reached sophomore year, you've already checked out, living on a diet of wheat bread and things with seeds, wearing Birkenstocks, and getting stoned) and Donald crushes Mallard by a better than two to one margin.

Today, nearly 20 years later, I drive up the road to the Oscar Getz Museum of Whiskey in Bardstown, Kentucky, with Steve Sandstrom, industrial designer, former fine arts major at the University of Oregon, and the creator of Mallard Drake, the man who will, as Arthur Shapiro has decreed, build the glass for Bulleit Bourbon. Steve, a certifiable eccentric, and I hit it off immediately. We both share a passion for working nonstop *"A weekend? What is that?"* a deep, unremitting commitment to excellence, and the same dry sense of humor, though mine, he insists, is clearly more Southern.

"What does that even mean?" I ask him.

"You don't have actual sarcasm," he says. "You have something more lethal because it sounds almost nice."

"What, just because we say 'bless her heart' after every putdown?"

"Something like that," Steve says, laughing.

* * *

Strolling through the Oscar Getz Museum, Steve takes in the history of bourbon like a student, but most often stops and considers the history of the *bottles*. A few times I catch him sketching in a small pad he carries. To this point, I've prepped Steve for the trip, giving him my copy of *The Social History of Bourbon*. I've taken him on the personal Tom Bulleit Kentucky Whiskey Tour—Keeneland Race Course, a distillery or two, my house, a cocktail with Betsy, lunch at Dudley's. We've talked Kentucky and we've talked *concept*.

"Of course, we want the bottle to match the concept," Steve says, after the museum, now looking out the passenger-side window at the rolling Kentucky countryside, speaking to me but thinking out loud. "As Arthur said, it has to look old. Authentic. It has to evoke the Old West. Augustus. I think—"

He stops, still gazes out the window.

"What?"

"It has to have your spirit. It has to tell your story." Steve turns and looks at me. "You know what I see? An old bottle with letters embossed on the glass. The words 'Frontier Whiskey' right *in* the glass. Letters you can touch."

"You can feel it," I say. "Literally."

"I've never made an advertising slogan the design," Steve says. "Too hokey, but mostly too short term." He pauses. "This might be the exception."

Later, Steve says he wants to go to antique stores and flea markets. I follow him like a puppy as he scours these places for old bottles. We find a few, but nothing that speaks to us, or I should say, to him. Finally, we decide to walk down the aisle of a local liquor store.

"Let's see what's in there and not use it," I say.

Arthur has decreed that the design be unique, that the bottle not look like anything else on the market. That Steve is to study every bottle, every label, of every brand of bourbon on the shelf. We slowly browse the bourbon aisle, pausing at each bottle, studying every bottle, every label.

"Which label do you love," Steve says, quietly.

I realize he's not asking a question. He's stating a fact.

"You know what? I love all these brands. I truly do." I smile at Steve. "When I decided to get into the bourbon business, the first person I called was Bill Samuels of Maker's Mark. I called not to get his permission, but to inform him of my decision, my career change, my life change. A courtesy call, you might say, but also, we're friends and I was excited. You know what he said? 'Tom, I think that's great. I wish you nothing but success. We're all family here. If it's good for bourbon, it's good for all of us. When the water rises, all the boats float higher.'"

* * *

Steve returns to his hometown, Portland, Oregon, and goes to work. He knows what he's looking for, sort of. He knows he's looking for inspiration and some kind of old bottle. He's just not sure *what* kind. He prowls through every antique shop in Portland, scouring shelves, poking through piles, combing through discards. Then, one day, in a stop in Southeast Portland, his eye goes to something sitting in a corner—a dusty, dark, olive-green bottle with an oblong body and a short, stubby neck. Steve approaches slowly, carefully, and picks up the bottle. *I like the color,* Steve thinks. *When you add the bourbon, the orange liquid will turn the glass black. It'll be weird, an optical illusion, and it will be very cool.*

Then Steve notices the bumps on the front side of the bottle. He rubs his thumb over them.

Embossed lettering, though not enough letters. Not as many as he envisions, but *Here it is,* he thinks. He turns the bottle over in his hands, feels its weight, considers its size. Smaller than what he needs, but this shape—

This shape would fit nicely into a saddlebag.

I can see it, Steve thinks. *It's 1850, some cowboy takes a draw from his bottle of whiskey, and tucks it back into his saddlebag.*

Frontier Whiskey.

Those words are no longer an advertising slogan.

Those words are vintage.

Those words tell Tom's story, Augustus's story.

Those words have to go on the bottle.

* * *

Steve looks at the short, stubby olive-green bottle on his desk, the one he purchased at the antique shop in Southeast Portland, and wonders—

Did bottles in the 1800s actually *have* raised lettering?

He does some research, finds vintage photographs, and discovers that craftsmen did make many bottles back then using three-part molds and thick glass, with cork stoppers and—*raised lettering.*

So—Frontier Whiskey.

I'm making something authentic, Steve thinks. *This is much more than an advertising slogan. This is real.*

Steve knows that the bottle he found in the antique shop isn't perfect, but its character assures him that he's on the right track. The bottle he stares at feels too chubby, too much an oval, shaped almost like an egg. He imagines that cowboy again, and this time sees him sliding an apothecary bottle out of his saddlebag, filled not with medicine but with bourbon.

He envisions the shape. He sees the glass—elliptical, short-neck, broad-shouldered. That's it. Without a doubt. Satisfied now with how he will shape the bottle, Steve gets to work on the lettering.

He begins fooling around with the layout, imagining what the embossing would look like. He copies some typefaces and cuts others out from vintage type catalogs he's collected over the years. One day, hunched over his desk, he meticulously positions each letter, slowly, carefully laying out by hand the words—B-U-L-L-E-I-T B-O-U-R-B-O-N in a slight arc, then below that, beneath a raised line—F-R-O-N-T-I-E-R W-H-I-S-K-E-Y with four raised dots below that, four periods, the letters all embossed.

Finished, he stares at his handiwork.

It feels intrinsic, as if it belongs, as if it has always been exactly this way. It fits. It feels—right.

Next, the label. He needs to create something that flows and that feels like an essential part of the bottle's identity. Again, in the simplest, most real way, it must fit.

Steve applies logic to the creative process.

He thinks, *I have to put aside my 1997 industrial designer self and pretend I'm a craftsman living in 1870, hired to make this glass.*

He sees the bottle. He looks at it. He holds it up to the light, turns it slowly in his hands. He lowers it, stares at it, frowns. He would never be able to wrap a long label around the tapered neck and oblong body. Well, he *might* be able to twist it all the way around, but if he managed that, the label would no doubt land on the front side at some sort of awkward tilt.

Yes, in order to make the label look as if it were applied by hand, the label would be askew, crooked.

So that's what it must be. Slightly flawed. Attached at an angle.

In addition, in order to remain consistent with the 19th century look, the crooked label would never match the embossed lettering on the bottle. The glass and the label would have been made in different trade shops and no doubt in different towns.

I'm not sure bourbon even came in bottles back then, Steve thinks. *I know the taste of bourbon had yet to be refined, as cowboys referred to their whiskey tasting like "coffin varnish."*

Steve designs the label—finding himself drawn to a golden-orange hue. He serrates the edges because he thinks that's the way it would have been done. He angles the label slightly and then, the finishing touch, he fills the label with copy, but keeps the label small, covering maybe a quarter of the front of the bottle. He positions the words "Bulleit Bourbon" and the slogan, the catchphrase, the logo, "Frontier Whiskey" on the front of the bottle *twice*—once on the label, and once embossed on the glass. And his final flourish, his crowning punctuation—he makes sure all you see is the liquid itself. Well, except for the label at the bottom, the tiny label, almost all. And he makes a statement. Given the deep olive-green color of the glass, adding the orange bourbon turns the color of the liquid in the glass a dark, murky, mysterious black.

"The production people are going to kill me," Steve says aloud.

And then he shrugs. "Oh, well."

When Steve finishes the dark green bottle, the bourbon appearing almost black, he studies what he has built, and he feels overwhelmed with triumph. He almost wants to shout in his office. Over the years, he's learned that when you succeed, you know it. You just—know it. *Same way I felt after I took the bar exam. I knew I nailed it.* Steve does, too.

*   *   *

"I love it," I say, absolutely floored by Steve's design, looking at the glass Steve has built, in a packed conference room at Seagram. "But is it a tad—dark?"

"Well, yeah, I know, because it would be back then, adding the orange bourbon to the green glass turns the liquid black. I mean, it's *authentic*—"

"I absolutely love the raised lettering, love the label, love it all. It's just kind of dark ..."

Steve sighs and, before I can say another word, a second prototype appears, one of four he's brought. This second one—the exact bottle, same embossed lettering—is clear. But when you pour the bourbon into this glass, an optical illusion occurs. It appears as if the bourbon, the golden liquid, is standing alone in mid-air. *You can almost touch the liquid*, I think. *Even better, you can almost taste it.*

Even *better*, you could sit on a barstool 15 feet away and identify Bulleit Bourbon just by the color, by the bottle, sitting on the backbar. You would not have to read the label. You would actually know the bourbon by its bottle. In addition, the orange label changes the color of the whiskey, bringing out the golden hue.

"Well, this is brilliant," I say, in a near whisper, moving my eyes from the bottle to Steve, and back again to the bottle. "Steve, you've surpassed … everything. What you've done here is iconic. It's *brilliant*."

"I was afraid you'd say that," he says, smiling through what I see is some combination of a true artist's pain and disappointment.

"You don't like it?"

"No, I do. I just prefer the dark green. It's so different. I imagine this mean, badass bottle on the backbar, the liquid almost black. It's cool and unique."

"I get it and I love that bottle, too, I truly do," I say. "But thinking commercially, it may be too dark."

"Frontier Whiskey," someone says, eyeing the embossed lettering on the bottle and then murmuring in ad-speak. "It's not a place, it's a state of mind."

Then, just as we had when Bob Mackell created the concept of Frontier Whiskey, we begin climbing the symbolic, proverbial pitch ladder from here, this conference room on the first floor, the bottom rung, ascending, we hope, to the top rung, Arthur Shapiro's office, in the penthouse. At each floor we receive the go-ahead to keep working our way up. At the top, Arthur beams at the prototypes. He's ecstatic, loves the orange liquid in the orange bottle with the tiny, tilted label. As Steve feels the tide shifting from his dark-green prototype, he says to me, quietly, "The only reason I made the label orange was because I thought it was going on the dark green bottle."

The celebration rages, the kudos continue, and then, inevitably, questions come, and people begin suggesting refinements, tweaks, so-called improvements. At one point, someone asks Steve, "The label is so tiny. How are you going to read it?"

Steve laughs, and says, "I don't have a good answer."

Everyone in the room laughs, Steve shrugs and says, "I guess you're going to have to look at the whole thing. The entire package. That was the idea, anyway."

"In other words, your *concept*," I say, which gets another laugh.

"I realize we're being extremely cautious, perhaps annoyingly so," Arthur says to the room, "but what we're doing here is actually rather momentous." He pauses, and then says, "You have to understand that this is the first start-from-scratch mold Seagram's has built in 35 years."

Two completely contradictory thoughts crash into each other in my mind—

Wow. They must really love this new product.

... and ...

Wow, they must have really hated the old bottle.

In the end, the Seagram brass allows research to choose the bottle. We offer four choices to focus groups and follow up with questionnaires and interviews, cull all that information, add our own informed opinions, and make our decision.

"We're going with the clear bottle," I tell Steve. "I know you're disappointed."

"No, I'm not disappointed. It's a preference, that's all." He holds for a beat. "Okay, I'm a little disappointed."

"You know what? Maybe I'll come out with a hundred proof or something and we'll go with the dark bottle."

"I like the clear bottle, don't get me wrong."

"Steve," I say, "you designed it. It's wonderful. Trust me."

"Tom, I do trust you."

A year later, Steve's design—the now iconic clear bottle with the embossed lettering begun, with Steve's reluctance, as an advertising concept—will win a Communication Arts Design award, beginning a run of awards, resulting in a shelf full of Golds and Double Golds for package design that the bottle will win nationally and internationally for years to come.

* * *

Time. I lose track of it. I lose myself *in* it. Mornings, I walk for exercise and to settle my careening thoughts and I imagine the events of the last few improbable years clumped together, barreling by.

Two years have gone by? I see, I re-enact, watching the events unfold again in a loop—September 30, 1997, after almost an entire year of back and forth negotiation, I sign the contract with Seagram; we go forward and create the "Frontier Whiskey" concept; we build the glass, the first new mold

Seagram has built in 35 years. Again, time, flittering away. So maddeningly elusive. I think how perhaps the most crucial part of making an excellent bourbon is all about time, the process you can't see at all—the aging in barrels. The weirdest mystery of life. We age, but we don't see it, at least not on ourselves. It just happens to us … and here we are. But now time roars by, and I watch some imaginary time lapse, months and years frantically flipping by in front of my eyes like a calendar in an old-fashioned movie. Suddenly we roar into the new millennium, the world holding its collective breath as we wait in dread for every computer in captivity to crash, for time to stop, for worldwide chaos to break out, for the world as we know it to end.

Of course, nothing remotely resembling that happens, except that here, in our tiny inch of the world *everything* happens in our own private millennium. We've changed our world. We've created the Bulleit Bourbon brand, and we're preparing to launch. We've used our time well, and although I consider myself a man of patience—I respect the power of waiting something out until you get it right and consider patience an action, not passive at all—I have at times felt my patience fray. I'm eager to roll out the brand. Because we've done it, and we've done it right, all of it, the theme, the bottle, the label—the *package*—and the golden liquid sloshing inside. I feel, not immodestly, simply truthfully, and with respect to every other bourbon on every liquor store shelf and on every backbar in every saloon in existence that we have created merely the best bourbon in the world. I honestly do.

During these past few years, while coming up with the new package, we've made some tweaks and refinements to the product. We've committed to distill our bourbon at the Seagram-owned distillery in Lawrenceburg, where we will finalize the bourbon's taste until we present Bulleit to the public in the form of Augustus's family recipe.

*   *   *

I want to get as close to Augustus's original recipe as possible. To work on the mash bill, which for the whiskey novices means simply the mix of grains, or, in English, the recipe, Seagram sets me up with a dream team—Art Peterson, the Master Blender for the House of Seagram, who's gifted with a top five in the world taster's palate; Neil Gallo, a kind of managerial wizard and professional human juggler, the man overseeing our entire project; Jim Rutledge, the master distiller; and me. Our purpose now, of course, is to do the math, get specific to the point of picayune, to come up with the *exact* equation. We're working with the general principle, Augustus's two-thirds corn, one-third rye family recipe, but that's just too vague. We have to go inside the numbers.

First, some history. At one time, in the mid-20th century, Seagram operated five distilleries in Kentucky. When bourbon fell out of favor in the Sixties and Seventies, Seagram shut down four of its facilities and consolidated everything at one distillery where the company, uniquely, made 10 different distillates using two mash bills and five patented yeast strains. The question arose: how to designate the whiskey when combined, as "Kentucky Straight Bourbon." Sam Bronfman, Sr., came up with a workable solution. He contacted the U.S. Bureau of Alcohol, Tobacco, and Firearms (B.A.T.F.) and proposed, essentially, that whiskeys made in the same still and combined be called "straight." This process would be called "mingled" and be in compliance with the requirements for straight whiskey.

Thus, mingling our various recipes we would be able to create our unique Kentucky Straight Bourbon Whiskey, which would be consistent from batch to batch from decade to decade.

*   *   *

We begin by experimenting with a number of recipes, searching for the perfect combination. With our driver, Augustus's family recipe, we stretch beyond the amount of rye content normally found in bourbon to a much higher rye content. After much trial and error, we eventually arrive at the following formula: 68 percent corn, 28 percent rye, and 4 percent malted barley, only a slight variation from Augustus's two-thirds corn, one-third rye. Now, having settled on the chemistry, we rely on Art Peterson's world-class palate. I believe in science, but the human palate is far more discerning. We're simply aiming for a perfect mix of taste and consistency, that's all.

And we find it. And it's perfect. It's not only perfect, it's perfect every time. Every single time, every single sip, every single taste. You define greatness by just that—consistency. Bobby Thomson did a great thing, once. In 1951, Thomson, a utility infielder for the New York Giants, hit a home run off the Dodgers ace Ralph Branca, a homer known as the "shot heard round the world," sending the Giants into the World Series. Great. Incredible. Magical. Some people call it a fluke.

On the other hand, Ted Williams of the Boston Red Sox hit .344 for his *career*, over 20 years, and in 1941 hit .401 for the entire season, remarkable, the last time a player hit over .400 for a season, a mere 79 years ago.

That's what I want Bulleit to be—the Ted Williams of Bourbon, unmatched, consistent, greatness poured into a shot glass, all the time, every time, every single time.

*   *   *

We prepare to launch. Playing it safe, Seagram decides to take it slow, to test the waters, to see how we'll play in four test markets before we go wide. As I say, I'm the world champion of patience, but now I'm antsy, and my morning constitutional walks make me even antsier as I start to once again calculate time passing. But I'm also confident in the package and the product and in Seagram, so I go along with the program. No. I *embrace* the program. Seagram has saved my financial butt and guided us to create a superb package. I am all in with them.

But …

I pick up—something. A strange vibe. An uneasiness. A nervousness. Something in the wind. We talk, all of us, the members of the team I've become so close with, and one day, Steve Sandstrom and I share a mutual moment of uncertainty. We've heard some crazy numbers tossed around lately, crazy *low* numbers, about the number of cases so far produced. I've heard the number 2,000, a number so absurdly low that I dismiss it. But I do wonder if what I've been hearing is right and that feeling, that vibe, concerns me and I express that concern to Steve.

"I don't know what's going to happen, Steve," I say.

"Meaning …"

"Meaning," I say, struggling to figure out exactly what I do mean, then blurt, "I love this brand, but I don't know if the brand will survive."

I will learn that I do sense something unsettling pulsing through the Seagram universe, but it has nothing to do with the Bulleit brand, or with me, at least not directly.

*   *   *

Marketing prepares to introduce the brand to our distributors. I'm not sure I'm invited, but I invite myself. I don't push my way in, I just offer to attend, promising I won't get in the way of anyone's sales pitch. I say, "It may not be a bad idea for me to come. You all are introducing Bulleit Bourbon. I am the Bulleit of Bulleit Bourbon. I'm Tom Bulleit. Might be interesting for everyone to meet me, to say hello. I'd certainly like to say hello to them. I'd like to circulate, shake a few hands, thank everyone."

I finagle my way into the room where it will happen, though I get the sense that the Seagram's sales team actually likes the idea that I'll be there, that as a policy they appreciate the personal touch, as long as I don't get in their way.

"I'll hang back, you won't even know I'm there," I say, trying to reassure anyone who registers an iota of a doubt, although none of these people have even an inkling of my competitive nature because inside me this thought bubbles and boils, *You get them in the room, you introduce the product, you get them interested, even slightly, and I'll close them.*

*   *   *

The vibe I feel previously morphs to rumor. My sources suggest that they've heard "things," rumblings, and that I'd better sit down, never a good sign, and then they say without saying anything specific that they hear massive changes lie ahead, seismic changes. I call my New York lawyers to get further information and they lay out the scenario they've heard. I really should sit down because what they tell me nearly knocks me down. They hear that Edgar Bronfman, Jr., has been considering a company overhaul. He begins to express publicly his dreams of becoming both a movie and music mogul. I'm shocked, and yet not surprised. I know Edgar to be a man of action, someone who like myself tends to go all in. I can't picture Edgar, Jr., dipping a toe in the water. I see him cannonballing into the deep end of the show biz pool, which I've heard is infested with sharks.

*   *   *

Seagram bestows me with a title, "Founder." I'm humbled by it and intend to live up to the name. At the meeting of distributors, the Seagram team introduces me warmly, and I circulate, making it a point to shake every-body's hand and remember everyone's name. I do this not out of some sense of duty or obligation, but because I want to. I'm genuinely interested in who will represent the brand, who will represent me. I want to have meetings like this regularly, and suggest that idea afterward. As I mingle, I feel a buzz in the room, an undercurrent of excitement. All the changes, refinements, tweaks, experimenting, in order to get the recipe exactly right, perfecting the taste, creating the package, taking the time it took to do that, was worth it. It was all worth it.

And then at the end of the first year of the millennium, heading into 2001, the Seagram rumor becomes reality. Edgar Bronfman, Jr., divests Seagram of all of its liquor holdings and uses the billions he accrues to buy a seat at the show business table. In fact, he pretty much buys a piece of the table itself. He purchases Polygram Music and Universal Studios. Pernod-Ricard and Diageo, two of the world's largest beverage compa-nies, buy Seagram's liquor holdings and divide the assets. Diageo acquires Bulleit, and to my satisfaction and great relief, assures me that they will keep intact the arrangement I'd negotiated with Seagram. I will remain the Founder, but now under the auspices of Diageo. Edgar Bronfman, Jr., changes the very nature of the Bronfman family business. He gets out of the liquor and beverage business and goes into the movie and music busi-ness. And I go into limbo.

Bulleit Bourbon in casks at the Shelbyville, Kentucky distillery.

Find Humility Before It Finds You

(Life Is Coming to Get Us All)

The 12 Apostles

I STAGGER INTO THE year 2001, feeling a blustery wind not at my back but in my face, a confusing, swirling wind, not the powerful gust that has in recent years propelled me forward. I feel unsteady, unsure of literally where I stand. The wind in my face lashes me, causing me to teeter and nearly topple, forcing me to grab on to the closest railing and hold tight while I steady myself and figure out my present and plan my future.

I have meetings with myself. These take the form of long walks alone or during silent, somber early morning workouts at the gym, or quiet meditations at my church. Yes, I pray. I pray for guidance and strength and clarity. I think about where I am, reflect on where I have come from, and contemplate where I want to go, where I know I *will* go, because truly and fundamentally, I have faith. Faith pulled me out of a foxhole alive. Faith gave me the strength and vision to start a crazy new career in my mid-40s without second-guessing myself. Too much. I'm confident now that faith will sort out the Seagram to Diageo handoff and show me the proper path.

I have to have faith because I have no money.

Seagram, I know, planned to nudge the Bulleit brand forward in baby steps, introducing our new look, new glass, new package as they

simultaneously tried to reintroduce the idea of bourbon itself. They envisioned a slow, steady build, starting in two markets, increasing to four, as
opposed to a buckshot approach, banging a mythological distribution button, propelling us to 60,000 cases across the country. *The proverbial tortoise
pace*, I think, and then I remember who won that race and that it wasn't
close and I feel marginally better.

The Diageo folks welcome me into the family, sincerely. *Falling uphill,
I continue to do that,* I think. Still, I get the sense that the company considers us at best a small brand, perhaps even a throw-in. They're a giant
beverage company, and they are well aware that current customers and
whiskey drinkers are not ponying up to the bar, ordering bourbon. Bourbon remains an afterthought. Hell, that's not accurate. Bourbon remains
so far off the radar it's not even a *thought*.

I consider my options, discuss with Betsy, a few close friends, and decide
to call Roger Witten, the lawyer who negotiated my deal with Seagram.

"You need Dan Squires," Roger says without hesitation. "Young guy
working for me. Summa cum laude at Harvard, editor of the *Law Review*
at Yale."

"Roger, I want someone with *credentials*."

Roger laughs, then says, "He's a good man, Tom. No, that's wrong.
He's the best."

"Roger, if you say so, then it is so."

I call Dan and we connect immediately. He turns out to be a tena-
cious warrior and an exemplar of common sense. He first points out the
obvious, making sure that I *see* the obvious, "Tom, you're going from Seagram, the all-time giant of giants, to Diageo, the largest player in your
universe. Someone up there likes you because you've been handed the
brass ring. Grab it."

"Oh, I'm aware. And I will grab the ring, count on that."

But a lawyer I am and always will be and, as I am both respectful of
and a stickler for contracts, I want to make sure that I will start at my new
company and my new arrangement amply protected. Simply put, I want
to start at Diageo with the same position that I had at Seagram. Dan and
his team monitor my contract, complete their review, and determine that
indeed Diageo will pick up my contract exactly. They've committed to
that, and Dan makes sure of it.

"In Diageo, you couldn't have a better partner," Dan says, one of the truest statements ever spoken, then and now.

To protect my interests, to review my contract, and to ensure that my transition from Seagram to Diageo is as painless as possible, I commit substantial capital to legal fees, but considering my angst, nervousness, and uncertainty, the amount feels more than fair. I loved Seagram, loved everything about the company and every person I encountered, from the security guard who greeted me in the lobby of their midtown Manhattan block-long building to every member of the Bronfman family. They embraced my brand, improved it, and saved my financial ass. I have a new family now, and I intend to love Diageo as well as I loved Seagram, and get them to love me back. Put it another way. I am my father's son. Nothing stops me. I keep moving. I keep plowing ahead. I will make it work at Diageo. I will make it my new home.

You must learn to deal with change. Not a suggestion, an imperative. Betsy will call my ability to adapt to change my greatest asset. I'll stop the narrative now and offer a word of advice to all entrepreneurs. Very simply—you need to be open to change because change is unavoidable and inevitable. If you can't adjust, you will drown.

And there is always a silver lining in the new garment, which may take time and analysis to identify, but it is there. Find it.

*   *   *

As we settle into Diageo, I ask about our advertising and marketing budget and I'm met mostly by smiles and shrugs and no actual numbers. Finally, someone drops the hammer. We have virtually no budget … as in a miniscule amount of dollars. At this point, Diageo will not allot any serious money to build our brand. They will commit to what's known in the trade as incremental dollars, meaning, the more the brand takes in beyond the meager amount that's budgeted—in clear English, if we exceed sales expectations and we have unanticipated profit (yeah, right)—the more the company will reinvest (give us) for advertising and marketing. We call this a paradox. In order to increase our sales, we need money for advertising and marketing. But in order to get more money for advertising and marketing, we have to increase our sales. This recalls for me Joseph Heller's classic *Catch-22*, the satiric, absurdist antiwar novel and the most accurate depiction of frustration ever written, or as I've put it variously to myself, Betsy, and God at separate times and in no particular order, "I'm screwed."

Too harsh?

Okay, I won't say I'm screwed, I tell myself. *That's a state of mind, a condition, doesn't get you anywhere.*

I pause in my assessment and say, aloud, "Let's just say I'm an afterthought."

Maybe so. But I'm not dead.

In the very beginning, I meet with as many sales reps and Diageo folks as I can. I see myself as needing to change both my way of thinking and theirs. I create a somewhat vague strategy, a game plan. I will gently, but firmly, push myself into the company's sightline. I will literally introduce myself to them and make them appreciate what they have with us. Make them see us. That's what we all want, always, to be *seen.*

It begins at home, I think. *Acknowledgment begins at home.*

"Diageo is my first customer."

I say this sentence aloud 100 times a day, to myself, to everyone working on my brand, to everyone within earshot. I repeat these words so often it becomes my mantra, my purpose, my battle cry.

One day, during the first weeks at Diageo, over a dinner in which I pick absently at my food, Betsy, knowing exactly what's eating me, asks, brightly, "So, how does it feel being the new kid?"

I grunt, rearrange my entrée with my fork and knife, study my plate as if it contains the secret to life.

"Put it to you this way," I say, finally. "For argument's sake, and I may be low, let's say Diageo has 2,000 priorities."

"Okay. For argument's sake, which priority are you?"

"Two thousand and one."

* * *

Diageo assigns Bulleit a Brand Manager, Chris Musumeci, a young Ph.D., eager, hardworking, and smart. Together we contemplate our goal: to get distribution in all 50 states. *Sell the brand.* To do that, we first have to convince the members of the Diageo sales force and our distributors to pick up Bulleit as part of their portfolio. Offering Bulleit is not an automatic. This is 2001 and the world's whiskey drinkers love vodka and scotch and have virtually no interest in bourbon. We have to change their minds, alter their perception, bring them kicking and screaming to the bourbon trough. We have to make them love bourbon, and Bulleit Bourbon.

"How are we going to do that, Chris?" I say one day, not rhetorically, cluelessly. "How are we going to get them to love Bulleit?"

"Maybe if people got to know you."

"Me?"

"Yes. You are Bulleit. You are the brand."

I see where he's going with this because, incredibly, I've arrived there ahead of him. I get that, instinctively.

As Larry Schwartz, president of Diageo North America, a bartender's son and grandson, will say, perfectly, "Tom, you can make anything. Selling it is the trick." He follows that up with, "Remember, first and foremost, we are in the relationship business."

I've identified and embraced that charge. Meet the sales force and our distributors, the bartenders, the store owners, and introduce Bulleit personally. Make appearances, make calls, knock on doors, have a drink, the personal touch, the old-fashioned approach. Meet. Greet. Converse. Engage. Be myself, be folksy? No. Be *myself*. Be real.

How do you do? I'm Tom Bulleit. Won't you try my bourbon? Try it. Take a sip. It's something, isn't it? In all modestly, I don't believe you can make a better bourbon. I really don't. Try another sip. Am I right? Now, let me tell you my story, how we got from there, way back there, in the 1800s, to here—

It feels crazy. Uncomfortable. Counterintuitive. Advertising builds brands, but not in this case.

Truth is, I don't know the first thing about sales. I'm just … me.

My parents raised me to be humble. They drilled this cardinal rule. *Ask about others*. Be interested in their lives, their stories. Don't talk about yourself. It's egotistical, not to mention, rude. But I realize—without doubt or hesitation—that for this enterprise to work, in order to shove my way through those 2,000 priorities and make the company take notice, I'm going to have to talk about myself all the time, 24/7. I don't want to; I am an introvert, a green-eyeshade lawyer, but I have to. It appears to be not only my job, but the key to our brand's survival.

It's even more than that. It's my makeup. My entire being. What drives me? Once again … *fear*. I live by fear. It will never go away. It hasn't yet and never will. I fear that I will fail, that I will disappoint, that I won't be able to pay my bills, that I will go bankrupt, that I will foreclose on my house because I can't pay the mortgage. I hear people talk about retirement and I stare at them as if they've gone crazy. Retirement? What the hell is that? What the hell is a weekend? I don't take days off. I have to work. I must work. I have no hobbies. I don't play golf, or tennis, or hang out at the country club. I work out every day, check in at church, read a lot, but *retire*? Incomprehensible. By the way, this whole notion of retirement is a relatively new phenomenon. Years ago, it didn't exist. If you retired, you starved. Imagine this conversation between a farming couple: "Well, I guess that's it, dear. The end. Think I'll retire. I'm not going to take care of the corn anymore."

If you don't take care of the corn, you'll starve. You always have to take care of the corn. There is no retirement. Retirement means death.

* * *

And so, Chris, Brand Manager, and I, assuming the role of Founder and Brand Ambassador, think out of the box and design an inside-outside strategy. I go from an entrepreneur to an intrapreneur. Chris coordinates my schedule both on the road and inside the Diageo building, pressing relentlessly for distribution priority while I address and entertain the key players within the company. I also become a lobbyist for budgets and markets, working it. I emphasize my story and show how much I genuinely care about my brand, and frankly, about them, the people I'm speaking to. We have to do this together, I say. We have a great story, but we have to write a new story, the story of how this little start-up brand grew, beginning right here, in this room. I think of us as the underdog who, despite all odds, fights every moment with a smile on his face to get into the game. I see myself as *Rudy* or *Rocky*. The brand that won't give up. That's who we are. That's how I feel. And that's what we will do.

And we have, as Arthur Shapiro said, a "360-brand."

But it's what I honestly feel. I express it this way to the people inside of Diageo—*One share of heart, one share of mind is more valuable than one share of wallet.* I feel that sentiment buzzing in these meetings. I feel the connection. Then I start to see results, tiny upticks, slowly at first, but I hear from Chris that the sales reps have begun including Bulleit as part of their portfolios, a huge deal for our miniscule brand. A sales person may rep 100 different brands, but will carry only eight sample bottles in his bag. Suddenly, I hear that he has replaced one of his sample bottles with Bulleit. I begin to hear variations of this: "I want to be part of the Bulleit growth story. I like Tom, I like the bourbon, and my customers love it. We're discovering something together."

Then I personally pound the pavement. I hit the road, three, four, sometimes five days a week. The first year, I log 200 days of travel, easy. I go on "ridealongs" with the sales folks and meet scores of people—sales force, distributors, store owners, clerks, bartenders, everyone remotely associated with Diageo, with our bourbon, with me. I talk to anyone who will talk to me. I don't try to guess who is likely to buy, don't try to identify obvious suspects. I may be wrong and miss a good bet. I do look for those with say-so, the people with obvious purchase power. But I consider no account too small, no challenge too big. I literally go door to door, bar to bar to bar, store to store to store, introducing my brand, my bourbon, myself. At first, I mostly hear one word, consistently, repeatedly: "No." Sometimes, though not always, that word is followed by two other words: "Thank you." I don't take the *Nos* literally. I consider a "No" as "I'm thinking it over" and if a bartender slams a door in my face or won't listen to my spiel, I take that as a "Not at this time" and I'll come back the next day and the day after that. I keep trying. I don't give up. I'll find common ground, something ...

"Mr. Bulleit, we're not interested in bourbon. Nobody's buying it."

"Oh, I know. But you haven't tried mine. It's different. A little heavier rye content. You're going to like it. Come on. Take a sip. Just one sip."

"Mr. Bulleit, really, I—"

"Tom. Call me Tom. I'm sorry, I can't help noticing ... that cap you're wearing. U.S. Navy. Did you serve?"

"Yes, I did, but—"

"So did I."

And I sit on the barstool in front of him and we begin talking Vietnam and our respective units and, before he knows it, he's pouring us both shots of Bulleit, and we're toasting that time we shared in the late Sixties and early Seventies, we share war stories, the ones we can share, and then we're connected, we're friends, with or without Bulleit, and along the way, sometimes he's sold.

I don't win everybody over. Especially bartenders, whom I love, but who can be tough. I get hard passes and am told to leave their saloons more than I would have imagined. But I record everything. I scribble notes on a pad, jot down addresses, names, milestones I may have gotten a bartender to mention, a birthday, anniversary, and after every meeting, every encounter, I follow up with an email exchange, a personal note, a thank you, a hope-to-see-you-again, especially for the hardest "Nos." Gradually, I see some results. An email I receive from a sales rep in Alaska makes me feel as if I doing something right. "Hey, Tom, I just sold a two-case display of Bulleit at this retailer in Anchorage. Just wanted you to know that I'm working hard for you."

I don't even remember going to Alaska, which gives you some idea of how much I'm on the road.

Around this time, I read and reread a seminal book for me, *The Tipping Point* by Malcolm Gladwell. Gladwell argues that a very small number of your workforce, in his estimation, 10 percent, will do 80 percent of all the work. If I buy into that theory—which I do—and apply that to myself within Diageo, I calculate that of a sales force of 100 people, 10 of them will provide 80 percent of my sales. Now the hard part. How do I identify those 10 people?

*   *   *

After the horrific events of September 11, 2001, the year comes to a slow, halting, unsettling end, but I gather myself up, and in the early months of 2002, I go back on the road with a renewed commitment and intensity. Work becomes my escape, my refuge, my therapy. Again, fear pushes me. *If I don't drive my brand, no one will.* That may or may not be a fact, but I believe it as fact and I work with an unsurpassed conviction. I don't relax, but I do sleep well, chiefly because every night after nonstop 12-hour days, I crash onto my bed usually in some hotel, exhausted, spent.

I head to the West Coast frequently, especially to San Francisco, a city I love, for both its intrinsic and architectural beauty and its culture. When

I can find a spare hour, I drop into museums, art galleries, Kuleto's, and of course, bars. Next to New York, San Francisco has become the center of a growing food and bar scene. Slogging through 2002, then going into 2003, I sense the start of something new, a deepening interest in the restaurant and bar culture, even what feels like the beginning of a culinary revolution. The San Francisco area has always been a center for groundbreaking restaurants—I think of Alice Waters's Chez Panisse in Berkeley and Thomas Keller's The French Laundry in Napa—but these places, while world class, exist on the outskirts of the city. A change is coming in the city, on the streets of San Francisco itself. And then I notice something else, another quiet rebellion.

I have for years flown my American flag proudly. But since September 11, 2001, I have noticed more and more American flags appearing every day on my neighbors' lawns, flying over garage doors, in car windows, and waving above their front doors. I feel a sense of newborn American pride, a sort of national unity, unlike anything I have ever experienced. The war I fought in, the Vietnam War, divided us as a country. But the attack on 9/11 has brought us together. Walking through Nob Hill, I wonder whether we're experiencing a kind of national pride even when it comes to eating and drinking. I do feel some sort of American craft revolution—a desire for craft beers, craft whiskeys, food grown locally, American farm to table, a celebration of different American cuisines. And what beverage could be more American than Kentucky Bourbon?

* * *

On one of my San Francisco trips, I meet Steve Beal, a man who will become my West Coast spirits/spiritual advisor and one of my dearest friends. Steve, passionate, highly energetic with a personality big enough to fill any room, including a concert hall, and an ordained Episcopalian priest, has become Diageo's first Master of Whisky, which sounds like a fancy title because it is. Diageo handpicked five Brand Ambassadors in the United States, brought them to Scotland, and had them trained in all the intricacies of distilling. The training turned out to be grueling and intensive and took years, ultimately costing the company millions of dollars. In the end, armed with certificates and an encyclopedic knowledge of spirits, Steve knew more about whisky—in particular scotch—than practically any person alive. He could work in a distillery and actually run the still, while wearing a kilt. I may not be right about the kilt, but I am 100 percent correct about the certification and the still.

When I meet Steve, we instantly connect. We talk religion and we talk bourbon. Turns out he—and I—have a passion for both. He has tasted Bulleit and has fallen in love.

"Before I met you and tried Bulleit, all I sold was scotch," Steve tells me. "Now, in my sample bag I have eight bottles, seven bottles of scotch, each priced more than $100, and one bottle of Bulleit, priced a lot less."

"Under $50," I remind him.

"Tastes twice that, easy," Steve says, and he's a priest, so I know he's telling the truth.

We talk whiskey, business, and books. We discover we've both recently devoured Malcolm Gladwell's *The Tipping Point*. The book has been on my mind lately because of conversations I've had with the highest echelon of the company—Paul Walsh, CEO of Diageo, Ivan Menezes, president of Diageo, North America, and Phil Gervasi and Jon Tepper, California's top brass. They all have expressed a strong commitment to building the Bulleit Bourbon brand. They only have one small caveat. They can't spend a lot of money on advertising and marketing. Their commitment is sincere and real, their charge absolute. They want this to happen. I have always seen Seagram as a family who brought me in, adopted me, in a sense. In the best way—and as a military man—I see Diageo as a well-oiled military family, a sort of branch of the British Navy. I see their top brass as admirals. I see myself brought into the fold with a lower rank, Chief Petty Officer or Midshipman. In any case, while Seagram felt like family, Diageo feels like home. As I've said, I love the military. I understand it and feel comfortable in it. In this case, I know that nothing can or will be accomplished without the admirals' orders. So here I am, in San Francisco, understanding their charge. I have their blessing and I have my orders—

Sink that ship.

Yes, sir. But sir, we don't have any torpedoes, how will we sink it?

That's your job, isn't it?

Yes, sir.

Figure it out, Tom, I tell myself.

June 17, 2019. Betsy and I in my office at the Grand Opening of the Bulleit Distilling Company Visitors Center in Shelbyville, Kentucky. I like to say that I'm always working and well supervised.

My dad and me in 1943 before he shipped out to join General Patton's Third Army in France during the 2nd World War.

1968, I Corps Vietnam, North Danang. I was a Corpsmen serving with the First Marine Division.

May 8, 2016 in Berlin for a market visit. Cheers!

November, 2019. The first iteration of the bottle for Bulleit Bourbon (left), designed by Meridian Communications, and the current design by Sandstrom Partners (right).

A 1999 ad for Bulleit Bourbon, framed at home in Kentucky. My favorite of the ad campaign, "When men were men and whiskey was bourbon," created by Bob Mackall and Jack Mariucci for Seagrams.

The ribbon cutting for Bulleit Distillery on March 14, 2017 –my birthday, the 30-year anniversary of my marriage to Betsy, and the 30-year anniversary of founding Bulleit Bourbon.

The sun sets over the distillery after the ribbon cutting ceremony.

The Bulleit Distillery Company.

Oct 3, 2018. The four Tattoo Edition bottles.

March 2018. Bulleit Bourbon in casks at the Shelbyville, Kentucky distillery.

June 11, 2019. Medals awarded to the Bulleit Brands by the San Francisco World Spirits Competition, the most prestigious competition for spirits in the world.

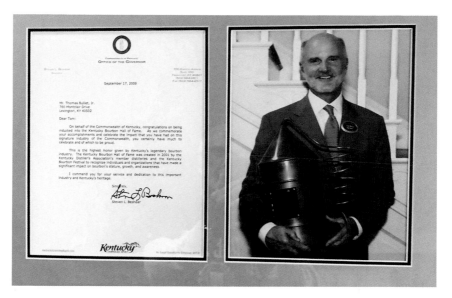

In 2009 I was inducted into the Kentucky Distillers Association Kentucky Bourbon Hall of Fame, the 59th person to be honored. To the left is a congratulatory letter from Governor Steven L. Beshear.

1997. Thomas Ewing (Tucker) Bulleit, III at home in Kentucky.

Spring 2015. Woodbine, GA. Me with my granddog Addison at the Seminole Cup Sporting Clays Championship, where Tucker was competing.

May 2019. Tucker and his pet, Luther T. Longhorn, on our farm in Bourbon County, Kentucky. Tucker raises angus cattle, non-GMO corn, and soy beans.

May 6, 2019. Betsy and her buddy Luther. Betsy was raised in Bourbon County about 5 miles from our farm. She was known as the Belle of Clintonville. Probably because she was the only one.

April 14, 2019. Hampden, our family dog, at home in Kentucky. Named for Tucker's alma mater, Hampden-Sydney College, because all love dogs who are family members.

May 29, 2016. Betsy and I in Normandy, France on a trip to meet with our French Brand Team in Paris.

October 22, 2016. Washington, DC at the National Architecture Museum for the 50th reunion of my graduation from Georgetown Law School.

Founders Two, me and Bill Samuels of Makers Mark, July 18, 2016

June 9, 2019. Me and Enrique de Colsa, master distiller for Don Julio, at the Apiary in Lexington, Kentucky for the United States finals of Diageo's World Class Bartender Competition.

November 15, 2019. Betsy with Hampden and his sister Sydney at the Bulleit Distilling Company for a photo session for the book *Bourbon Tails*.

November 2019. The Joe Club is a man cave/office over our garage in Kentucky, and I have this pinned to the wall next to my desk. The Quiet Hero, Gregory Peck as Atticus Finch, inspired many of us to go into law and work for justice.

November 2019. This is the Martin G. Hanse, Sr. Humanitarian Award I received in 2016 for my support of the Semper Fi Fund, which helps wounded Marines.

I was honored to be the 22nd inductee in the Hometown Hero program, which began in 2002. The program features notable Louisville natives, including Muhammad Ali, Colonel Sanders and Diane Sawyer.

August 3, 2019 at Cars & Coffee in Lexington, Kentucky. A common interest I share with my beloved son Tucker. "Family First."

February 5, 2017, Valley of Fire State Park, NV. Me, Elissa Lafranconi, Betsy, and Francesco Lafranconi. We traveled to Las Vegas for a market visit and to spend time with my friend Francesco, who is one of the most famous bartenders in the world.

Greetings from Valley of Fire State Park

August 8, 2014 on a market visit to Seoul, Tokyo, and Jakarta. Pictured in front of the Johnnie Walker House in Seoul.

Be creative. Be resourceful.

It's simple. It's just not easy.

* * *

Steve starts us off. He pitches an idea he calls the California Plan, growing the brand through bartenders, bar to bar, in the bourgeoning cocktail culture in San Francisco.

"I love talking to bartenders," I say, which is true, but it's also true that I will sell our bourbon to anyone who will listen. A few nights later, we have our first major meeting at Diageo headquarters in San Francisco. The company packs the building with what feels like the entire population of Northern California. I don't know every person in the room, but I shake every hand, take down as many names and emails as I can. At one point, late in the evening, when most of the attendees have left, I stand talking with a man in a pale blue shirt who smiles and nods often and enthusiastically.

"Very nice meeting you, Rolando," I say, pumping his hand, as Gene Song, our new Brand Manager, comes up behind us. "We'll be in touch."

Rolando nods, smiles, shakes Gene's hand, and leaves.

"Nice guy," I say to Gene.

"Yeah," Gene says. "I think he's the janitor."

I shrug. "He likes bourbon. I think. He doesn't speak English. But, hey, one bottle at a time, right?"

The next day, walking toward my hotel in the cool San Franciscan afternoon with Steve Beal, we talk further about *The Tipping Point*, and referring to a concept in the book, discuss how we can identify our mavens and connectors, as Gladwell calls them, people who can "tip" Bulleit from an obscure, little known bourbon to a brand everyone will know. We talk about offering an incentive to the top sales reps, distributors, even to the most influential bartenders in the Bay Area. Steve calls these people our "key adorers." Our brand, at sales of 20,000 cases or fewer, still tiny, continues to receive virtually no money for marketing. We have to be resourceful and creative.

"What do other companies do for their top people every year?" Steve asks in a way that suggests he already knows the answer.

"Trips," I say. "Cabo. Vegas. Hawaii. Golf resorts. Glitz. Glamour."

"Exactly. Great incentives. Wonderful locales. Exotic. We, of course, can't afford any of that. So, what do we have and what can we afford?"

"Okay, I'll play along," I say. "Nothing?"

"No," Steve says. "Incorrect. We happen to have a very, *very* effective asset, something we can offer."

"What?"

"You."

"Me?"

"You. Everybody loves you. Even better, everybody wants to spend time with you. They want to hang out with you. You're accessible, available, you're funny, you're charming. But there's just so much time you can spend with each person. So ... we make *more* time for them and you. We give them an opportunity. We'll take them on a pilgrimage. We'll bring them to Mecca."

"The Middle East?"

He looks at me, laughs, and then I laugh and say, because I do understand where he's going. "Kentucky. We'll bring them to Kentucky."

"Right. Show them where it's done and how you do it."

I nod, taking in the idea.

"I don't know," I say.

But I feel a creative spark, something that ignites, and I feel with more thought, revision, and coordination with the folks at Diageo this could work. It makes sense. I remember when I brought Steve Sandstrom and Bob Mackell to Kentucky and took them on my personal tour, showing them *my* Kentucky, and how enamored they both became of my home state. In subsequent conversations, bringing in Gene Song and others from Diageo, we get more specific.

"We have assets here," I say. "We can take them to Keeneland Race Course. The Bluegrass Sportsman's League to shoot sporting clays. The Iroquois Hunt Club on Boone Creek. Our home."

Then I bring up our secret weapon.

"And Betsy," I say. "No one is a better host—or hostess—alive. She has a gift for entertaining. I'll be there. But I'm window dressing."

I pause.

"Frankly, we can't do a trip like this without her," I say.

I begin to think it through, and then I start to *see* it, as if the family trip already exists.

"I'll bring them *home*," I say. "Literally. I'll bring them to my house, have them meet my family, Betsy, see the old photographs, Augustus. I can have a real down-home Kentucky barbecue, maybe take them riding, and then we can visit, spend actual time together. It won't be glitzy, but it'll be *us*."

"It'll be unlike anything out there," someone says.

"A Kentucky family trip," I say. "Not to mention, it'll be pretty inexpensive."

I pause.

"It'll be personal," I say, then adding one of my most important Bulleit Points, paraphrasing Larry Schwartz, "All business is personal."

And so, we birth the Bulleit Family Trip, which has become, over the years, one of our top marketing events. Since that first trip, bringing groups to Kentucky of between 15 and 45 people at a time, we have hosted more than 3,000 sales people. Over 125 groups.

*   *   *

The revolution begins.

It happens quietly at first, so quietly we're not sure it happens at all. But it does and, once again, Steve Beal is at the heart of it. I see it as the moment Bulleit breaks out. But unlike most revolutions, this one begins with mixology. In San Francisco.

Steve knows a bartender, Jon Santor, in the Mission, at Bruno's. Right now, he may be the only bartender in all of San Francisco who serves Bulleit. Jon is a mixologist, but prefers to be called a bartender. I will ultimately accuse Jon of entrepreneurship (see "Prizefighter" bar in Oakland).

Steve picks a day and invites 11 of his favorite bartenders—the top 11 in the city—to join us and the 12th bartender in the backroom of his bar for mixology and bourbon.

"You'll like Jon," Steve says as we walk into the bar. "He's the only guy I know in the city who's pouring Bulleit. But that's not why I like him. I like him because he's very knowledgeable, inventive, creative, a bartender's bartender. That's literally what people call him."

"A partner in chemistry," I say.

Steve laughs. "I like that," then claps his hands. "Okay, everybody, let's make some cocktails."

Within minutes, we're sitting in the backroom of the bar, sipping cocktails Jon and a couple other bartenders have concocted, laughing, downing burgers. For most of these bartenders, maybe for all of them except for Jon, this is their first introduction to Bulleit, and to me. They love the bourbon straight and, as I've been preaching for a decade, they love using Bulleit as a mixer. The bartenders experiment. They love the high rye content of the bourbon, which brings a dryness that expands the spectrum of creative opportunity. We all taste. When a cocktail works, I see their pride and their commitment to their craft. I identify with them. They take their work seriously. They're not just doing this to make a living. It's much more than that. They consider themselves, at the least, craftsmen, and in some cases, artists.

"For me, this is not a job," one tells me. "It's my career. It's who I am."

I take their names, their contact information, and hours later, as Happy Hour approaches and the backroom darkens, each one has become a friend.

"That was great," I tell Steve later.

"It was," Steve says, "and we converted all of them."

"To my new religion, mixology and Bulleit. They go well together, by the way. Steve, I want to make this a regular tour stop."

"Like Alcatraz," Steve says, laughing, and then he gets strangely solemn. "You know, at one point, I looked over at you and these 12 bartenders, these 'adorers,' these mavens, and you know what I saw?"

"What?"

"Jesus and his disciples."

"That's a tad too far, don't you think?"

Steve doesn't hear me. He's on a roll.

"Twelve bartenders," he says. "The 12 Apostles."

Then Steve looks at me and grins.

"Something started here today."

"In a bar. With burgers and Bulleit."

"The 12 Apostles," Steve says again. "I'm telling you."

And so, although neither of us knows it yet, we have kicked off the revolution. In short order, the 12 apostles will bring Bulleit to their bars, introduce the bourbon to their bosses, put Bulleit on their menus, and bring it to the attention of their customers. The apostles will literally spread the word, the word being Bulleit. That word will start to propagate, slowly at first, then faster, louder, more insistently as the 12 apostles themselves will move on to other bars, in other cities, preaching the gospel of Bulleit, embracing the concept of bourbon as a cocktail spirit. Then the subtle expansion of the brand will move to a tipping point when one of the apostles, Jon, now managing a speakeasy, "Bourbon and Branch," in the center of San Francisco's cocktail culture, will invent a new drink at the request of Bobby Dowgiallo, our salesman on his first day on the job, that will cause Bulleit Bourbon to explode. He'll call the cocktail the Bulleit Revolver. We'll never look back. In the end, the revolution will take years, but that's how some revolutions go.

Plan Ahead

(If You're in the Far-Left Lane and You Need to Exit Right in 500 Feet, You May Arrive in the Afterlife Instead of Altoona)

Bourbon in My Blood

March 14, 1953

I AM 10 YEARS OLD TODAY.

I feel the same today as I did yesterday, still Little Tommy, running harder and biking faster, sometimes, than the other kids my age, and taking the lead when we play "Army." But in some ways, I feel—different, older, more serious, more adult. Maybe it's because I've made it into double figures. I'm ready to say goodbye to parts of childhood. I won't miss being a *kid*. In fact, some older folks call me *an old soul*. I'm not sure what that means, but I would like to stay up later, read books, cross the main street at the bottom of our hill on my own, carry a jackknife.

That afternoon, Mother calls me into the kitchen. When I come in, she sits at the table, her hands folded in front of her. I pause in the doorway. She nods at the chair across from her.

"Sit down with me," she says. She smiles, but I see through it. She never invites me to sit with her at the kitchen table, just the two of us. This is our regular gathering place, where our family eats breakfast, the four of us, Mother, Dad, Mary Jo, and me. We use the dining room, a few feet away, for dinner only.

"Sit down, Tommy," Mother says.

This can't be good, I think. I rack my brain trying to picture my latest transgression or misdemeanor, possibly something she knows but I don't, and I draw a blank. I can't come up with anything that would warrant a private kitchen sit-down. If I've really messed up, committed a felony, I'd find my father sitting here, or he'd summon me to the living room where I, the guilty party, would face him as he sat in his armchair about to mete out my punishment. My head down, at a loss, moving in slow motion, I take the chair across from my mother. She smiles wider, fidgets, clears her throat.

"You're 10," she says.

I nod. That much I know.

"You're adopted," she says. "You know that, of course."

I look up at her.

"Yes," I say.

I've known that for as long as I can remember. My parents have not only informed me from the earliest age I could process the information that I had been adopted, they have embraced the idea. I am, they say, a blessing and even more than that, I know that my parents have personally selected both me and my sister. *Chosen children*, my parents call us. In fact, *I* helped choose my sister. I carry a distant, vague memory of walking with my parents into Our Lady Home, where my parents adopted me, and selecting, with them, my sister, Mary Jo.

Mom, Dad, and I enter a large, institutional room with pale walls and floors. I have an image of a church, high ceilings, a crucifix to the front, and before us a center aisle splits the room. We walk down the aisle, lined on both sides with cribs. My parents and I wear our winter coats and we walk slowly, heavily, my head swiveling from side to side, my eyes scanning over the babies in every crib. As we walk, a shimmering gold light streaming through slats in Venetian blinds blankets the room. We walk down that aisle, a baby occupying every crib, each one fast asleep, the putter of his or her soft snoring at our backs, sweet, magical music.

We come to the end of the aisle and, one baby not asleep at all, the last baby, is standing up, her tiny fingers gripping the side rail of her crib. The baby sees us and dips her chubby legs slightly, and smiles. Then she looks directly at me, gives me a coy grin, and smiles wider. She snorts and practically laughs. I can't help myself. I crack up. Then I look at my parents, who smile back at me. I want to reach over and pick up this baby, knowing, of course, that she is my sister and we have to take her home. We have made our selection. I realize later, of course, that my parents have picked her out before, but I'm thrilled that we have all settled on the same baby. We don't take Mary Jo home that day—a paperwork snafu or a minor illness keeps her at Our Lady Home for a few more days—but I leave knowing that I have helped choose my baby sister, that she will come home with confidence, a good nature, a ready smile, and a mind of her own, and that I love her already.

In the kitchen, my mother shifts her position in her chair, unfolds her hands, and rests her palms on the table.

"I wanted to ask you." She halts for a moment, then says, "Would you like to know about your birth parents? I know quite a bit about your mother, but not much about Mary Jo's."

I take a deep breath. My mother has never before mentioned my birth parents, never acknowledged their existence.

"Mary Jo has asked about her birth parents, more than once, actually. She's very interested. I thought, then, that you might also—"

I drop my eyes, stare into the table. My mother tilts her head. "So, if you wanted to know—"

I look up from the table, lock into my mother's eyes.

"No," I say, louder than I mean to. "I don't ... I don't want to know."

I drop my eyes again, trying to identify the powerful, insistent emotion I feel.

Disloyalty, I realize.

I feel disloyal to my parents.

I know my father. I know my mother. They are my parents. They always will be. My *mother*—my only mother—sits across the table from me now, as she does and has every single night of my life. I'm not interested in knowing any other mother.

My mother reaches over and takes my hands.

"Well, if you ever want to know, just ask," she says, softly.

I nod, absently, lift myself up from the table and practically run out of the room.

* * *

I don't really think about my birth mother again until a few years later when my mother once again tells me that Mary Jo has been wanting to know about her birth parents and asks if I'd like to know mine. Feeling the same sense of disloyalty as I did when I turned 10—disloyal to her and my father—I again tell her that I'd rather not know anything about my birth parents. *I'm fine not knowing. I don't want to know.*

I don't think much about my birth parents for at least 25 more years when I'm standing in the middle of a scrum of sweaty people at the local post office, applying for my first passport. Finally, after what seems like a week of waiting, a clerk, a wrinkled, bespectacled senior citizen in a rumpled blue uniform who looks like my old high school English teacher, calls me up to his window.

"Passport," I say, sliding him the application and handing him my driver's license. The clerk stares at my license for a long time, frowns back at my passport application, sniffs, looks up at me, adjusts his glasses, sniffs again.

"I know," I say. "I'm in my thirties and applying for my first passport. Ridiculous, right? It's true. I haven't traveled anywhere. No fun trips, no exotic places, no overseas vacations. Well, Vietnam, but I wouldn't call that fun, and certainly not a vacation. And I didn't need a passport."

"Thomas Ewing Bulleit, Jr.," the clerk mutters, scowling at my passport application. He scratches his cheek, squints at me through his thick eyeglass prescription, hunches over the form, and stares back up at me.

"Is there something wrong?"

"I'll be right back," the clerk says, slouching toward a door behind him, labeled "Administration."

I settle in, waiting for what seems another week, and then the clerk returns, shaking his head, looking even more grim-faced than before.

"We have a problem" he says.

"Okay ..."

"You don't exist."

I blink. "I'm pretty sure I do. I'm standing right here."

"I did some checking and you are not Thomas Ewing Bulleit, Jr. You are, in fact, James Howard Simpson."

I'm not sure what to say or what to do, so I just stare at the clerk, my ability to speak momentarily absent.

"Do you know you're adopted?" the clerk says, quietly, helpfully.

"Yes. I do."

"Well, James Howard Simpson is the name your birth mother gave you."

"I didn't know."

"Yes, that much seems clear."

"But my legal name ..."

"Yes," the clerk says, waving his hand as if swatting an invisible fly. "Bulleit."

He sighs as if he's just hauled a hundred-pound weight on his back up a steep hill. "We'll fix it."

He goes back to the "Administration" area. Now, I sigh. And while I wait for him to sift through the appropriate paperwork, make the required adjustments, and finally issue me my first passport, which he does, I make two life-altering pre–New Year's resolutions.

First, I resolve to travel more.

I start soon, my new passport in hand, eventually logging more than three million miles, traveling the world.

Second, I resolve to maybe be open about my birth parents some day.

I do that, too.

Takes me 15 more years.

* * *

After my parents have both died, Mary Jo embarks on a mission. She decides to find her birth parents. Her quest begins when she opens our dad's safe deposit box and finds an envelope with the words "Mary Jo's Adoption" written on it. Inside the envelope, she finds papers, perhaps her birth certificate—and a folded paper with her birth mother's name.

She then begins following the clues, becoming a detective solving a case, often blocked by sudden obstacles, but never quitting. My sister's and my adoption had both been closed adoptions—meaning the birth parents' names had been changed to protect their real identities—and Mary Jo realizes she needs help to continue her search. As Mary Jo chases clues down a series of dead ends, she sees that she needs someone with experience, a closed-adoption detective.

She somehow comes upon Roger Futrell, a state employee with a decades-long interest in genealogy who over many years has developed a passionate and perhaps unusual hobby: finding birth parents, even when they've been protected by closed adoptions. He offers to help Mary Jo. She refers to him as a professional searcher. After a surprisingly short time, he locates her birth mother, a nurse living near Boston. During one of our frequent phone calls, Mary Jo tells me this new information—she has contacted her birth mother and plans to visit her. Then Mary Jo goes quiet on the phone.

"I found your mother, too," she says.

"What?"

"I have found your birth mother," Mary Jo repeats, patiently, as if I hadn't heard her.

"I didn't ask you to do that," I say.

Once again, I feel that rush of loyalty toward my parents, as if my sister's finding out my birth mother's identity serves as some sort of threat to my mother's memory. I haven't raised my voice to my sister, but I've been short with her, pretty much dismissed her offer. I've instinctively and irrationally taken on the role as my mother's protector, a role she never would have wanted—or needed.

Mary Jo, though, persistent, strong-willed, presses on. "Oh, okay, fine, you don't want to know. Now. But if you ever do—"

"I'll let you know," I say.

Ice.

"Okay," Mary Jo says.

But for some reason, I can't shake the thought. My mind lingers on Mary Jo's search.

"How? I mean, how did you find her?"

"Roger Futrell. He's the guy who helped me find my birth mother. He thought it would be pretty easy, given the information Mother had, and so I went ahead, just in case you wanted to know. We're not positive, but given that we knew Aunt Sister Jean Clare was your stork, it seems very likely, almost definite, that your mother was her student."

Aunt Sister Jean Clare. My father's sister. Former graduate student who became a teacher and then a nun. Some called her "Top Nun," dean of women at Nazareth College in Louisville, superintendent of St. Peter's Orphanage in Memphis, and head of Adoption Services in Roanoke, Virginia. I remember Jean Clare as sweet, soft-spoken, and gentle, unlike her sister, Pearl. Aunt Pearl—had she gone into the convent I would've called her "Attila the Nun"—once tried to talk sense into me during my wayward party days at the University of Kentucky. She failed.

"My mother was her sister-in-law," I say, with a hint of defiance.

"I mean your birth mother."

I say nothing. I have said enough. Mary Jo knows that. She knows me.

"If you want to know more, let me know," she says.

"I will," I say.

* * *

I tell Betsy about the conversation, assuming that she's on my side. "Can you believe my sister? She goes ahead and finds out about my birth mother and doesn't even ask me. What nerve. Uncalled for. Right?"

Betsy gives me one of her looks that falls somewhere between a shrug and an insincere smile, meaning, I've learned, over time, that she thinks for herself.

"I take it you don't agree," I say.

"I understand your reluctance, and I respect that, but there is another issue. We don't know anything about your health history. It might be helpful to have a medical record."

"Well, I see your point. When you put it like that."

"I'd just kind of like to know if you're going to drop dead tomorrow so I can prepare my future. You know what I mean?"

She smiles, kisses me on the cheek, and breezes out of the room.

Of course, she's right. But I'm not going to tell her that. I can't give her the satisfaction of knowing that I know she's right, that she's won.

Then, alone in my office, I wonder—how many of these matrimonial skirmishes have *I* won?

Not that many, I think. *I bet I can count them on one hand.*

I stare at my hand, ready to tick off all my winning arguments. I extend my thumb. I draw a blank.

"There has to be one," I say aloud.

"One what?" Betsy says from the other room.

"Nothing," I say, which is both the answer to her question and the total number of matrimonial wins I can come up with.

Betsy's right, I say to myself. *I probably should find out about my birth mother—for my medical history.*

I resolve to do that. And I do.

Takes another three years.

* * *

Diverticulitis.

A funny word. I recall roaring at Gilda Radner mangling the word and all its syllables on *Saturday Night Live*.

Then I get hit by my own particularly nasty case of it. While the word diverticulitis may be hilarious, I wouldn't call the condition itself funny at all. The word *brutal* comes to mind. After I recover, Betsy insists that I go in for a complete physical and, before I realize it, we've picked up on the adoption conversation from three years ago.

"You'll be asked to fill out your medical history, Tom," she says. "It might be helpful if you actually knew what it was."

I sigh, nod, give her a look, say nothing.

"Seriously, it would be good to know if you have a history of heart issues, diabetes, cancer, whatever. We could watch for these things."

I sigh again, this time not in frustration, but in resignation. Yes, I know she's right. Again. My losing record remains intact. On our matrimonial scorecard, I remain winless.

* * *

It still takes some time for me to muster the nerve or the resolve or to convince myself to make the move, but a week or so later, I call Mary Jo.

"Okay," I say. "Who is she?"

"Who is *who?*"

"My birth mother."

"Well," Mary Jo says, softly, "I thought you'd want to know. Eventually." She pauses, and then she says, her words rushing out, "Roger and I think it is Mrs. Orline Ballard in Bardstown. We have lots of clippings about the family. It's a large family, 12 kids. We think she was a nursing student at Nazareth College when Aunt Sister Jean Clare was Dean of Women. We don't know who your birth father is."

I swallow and grip the phone tighter. I try to speak, but I can't formulate any words. I feel my pulse quicken.

"Are you there?"

I nod.

"Tom?"

"Yeah. Yes. I'm here."

"Are you …?" Mary Jo holds, then says gently, "Do you want to call me back?"

"No," I say, the word stinging. "No. I'm okay."

In silence, we hang on to the line, to each other, and then finally, I'm able to say, "If I wanted to, you know, meet her, or something, what would I do?"

"Write her a letter."

"Yeah, a letter. That's a good idea. Maybe I'll do that." I pause. "What would I say?"

I don't think Mary Jo has prepared the answer to this question in advance, but it almost feels as if she has. As usual, she seems to know exactly what to say, in a burst, word for word.

"Say 'I think you and I met on March 14th, 1943, and I would like to renew our acquaintance. You may be interested to know I have a daughter studying in France and a son here in Kentucky. My address in Lexington is …, and my home phone number is … Please write me a letter or give me a call. I would much appreciate it.' Sign it, you."

"You just dictated the whole thing."

"I know."

"Thank you," I say, nodding absently at the phone. "And thanks for finding out everything."

"It's okay. And Tom?"

"Yes?"

"Write the letter."

*   *   *

I write the letter almost as soon as we hang up, pretty much transcribing Mary Jo's dictation word for word, seal it, mail it. Twenty-four hours later—I'm shocked that the mail in Lexington moves so fast, for I have a kind of premonition—the phone rings. Sitting in my office, the jangling ringtone drills into my head, sounding twice as loud as usual. I look at the phone and I freeze. In my periphery, I see Betsy enter the room, and answer the phone. She peers at me, then walks over to me, her hand cupping the phone.

"It's for you, Tom," she says. "I think it's your mother."

I take the phone from her, my mouth opening and closing silently as she leaves the room. I look at the phone in my hand and study it as if it's some foreign object I've seen for the first time, then I slowly bring the instrument to my ear.

"Hello," I say.

"Hello, this is Orline Ballard."

The slight, whispery voice of an older woman echoes in the silent room, then after a three-count, she says, "I'm your mother, Tom."

"Thank you for calling," I say.

And then I freeze again.

I wanted this. I called my sister. I asked her to tell me about my birth mother. I wrote the letter. I asked my mother to call me. I mailed the letter. I did all of this willingly, knowingly, purposefully.

And now I feel completely unprepared for this moment.

I'm stunned, as still and cold as a statue.

I grip the phone, my knuckles turning white. I don't consider hanging up. I don't consider—anything. I simply feel at a loss. I feel myself inhale, then exhale, long and slow, taking some kind of cleansing breath, and then without thinking, totally by instinct, as if I am someone else and somewhere else, hearing myself in the distance—I begin to speak. The words burst forth out of my mouth—and from deep in my heart.

"Thank you," I say, and then I say, softly, insistently, "I want you to know that you did exactly the right thing. You made the right decision." I pause, and feeling a kind of heat, my previously frozen self, melting, I say, "I have had a wonderful life. My parents could not have loved me more or provided for me better. They instilled in me a deep faith and provided me with a wonderful education. I am a lawyer and I have on occasion represented women placing their children for adoption and also parents who have adopted children. I know that giving up a child for adoption is one of the hardest decisions a woman can make. But it is also one of the best decisions a woman can make. We have an adopted son, Tucker, and I thank God every day for his birth mother's decision."

I hear Orline Ballard, my mother, sigh, and then I hear another sound. A muffled whoosh of breath and then I hear what sounds like a small gasp.

"I just want to say again, I want to emphasize, that you chose exactly the right people and right parents for me. They were so, so special. I cannot tell you how much I appreciate what you did."

I hear the sound again, that tiny gasp, and I realize that my mother has sighed in relief.

"Thank you," she murmurs, with a kind of—reverence, almost in prayer, and I suddenly understand her subtext. I realize that without speaking words, she has asked me for something.

She has asked me for forgiveness.

I know now that she has been living with guilt, and in pain, and she wants to be forgiven.

I can't do that.

I don't have the ability nor the right to forgive. It's not in my power. It's well above my pay grade. No matter what I say, I know she will have to find the fortitude to forgive herself. But I can tell her again, without hesitation, and with total conviction, that I know she did the absolute right thing—for me, and for my parents. And in this moment, I know something else, something without doubt, something deeply spiritual.

I will believe to my dying day that somehow God spoke through me, enabling me and empowering me to tell my birth mother that she *had* done the right thing and that she should be forgiven and that she has to forgive herself. I believe that God has made me the messenger. He has told me to tell her. I never planned what I would say to her, never rehearsed the words or thoughts I would express to her, never gave what I would say a nanosecond of thought. The words spilled from me unchecked, gushing as if from some larger, preordained source. I believe that. I believe that God wanted His beloved daughter to know that she had done the right thing and that she should now commit to spend the rest of her life in peace. Otherwise, I cannot explain where my thoughts came from. I had never considered my law practice relevant to my adoption, never gave a moment's thought to my son's adoption having any relevance to mine. I spoke those words—those truths, those mercies—to my birth mother. They came out of my mouth. But they came not from me. Then my mother reveals something that levels me.

"I'm 82 years old, Tom," she says. "I want you to know that I have prayed for you every day. Every day of your life. The children always ask me, 'Why 13 rosaries?' You, Tom. You're lucky thirteen."

"I would like to meet you," I say.

"And I would like to meet you."

"Tell me when it's convenient for you and I'll be there."

"Come to Bardstown next Tuesday at noon. We can finally spend some time together."

*   *   *

Bardstown, Kentucky, the second-oldest town in the state, has been named by both Rand McNally and USA Today as the "Most Beautiful Small Town in America." A small, quaint town surrounded by puffy green hills, a tree-lined main street, at various times home to 40 distilleries, a featured kickoff point on the Kentucky Bourbon Trail. I spent my childhood traveling between Louisville and Bardstown, visiting my Uncle Bob Heaton, and Aunt Jody, my godmother. Summers, I swam in the public pool and played baseball at the park with the local kids. I know this town, even though I haven't spent much time back here. I think of Bardstown now and I see a lush, hilly, thriving little town, and I recall, sadly, more than a dozen young men who left for Vietnam and never came home. Lately, I haven't had much call to make the hour-drive from Lexington, until now.

I take the Bluegrass Parkway, more of a truckers' highway than the cozy two-lane back road the name suggests, and arrive at Mrs. Ballard's townhouse at exactly noon. I am obsessively early by nature but this particular meeting feels like one I need to arrive at neither too early nor too late. I fidget at her front door, hesitate, and for a fleeting moment, I ask myself, "Tom, what are doing?" and then I shake it off and jab the doorbell with my thumb. Almost immediately, the front door swings open and a woman a few years younger than me appears, her face round, full, flushed, and filled with a joyous grin.

"Tom, hello, I'm your sister, Sally."

She leads me into the living room where I meet Dee, another of my sisters, and then I stand face to face with a slight, frail woman sitting on the couch, a pair of reading glasses and rosary beads on the end table by her elbow. Sally stops and gestures toward her.

"And this is Mom."

The next moment blurs. I see my mother's lip tremble and as I walk to her and take her hands and she stands to meet me, I at once see the resemblance. I have her nose, chin, eye shape, eye color, and slender, wiry build. We're not identical, by any means, but I see myself in her. And as I clasp her hands in mine, and we hug, I feel blessed. Only that. Blessed. After I told Mary Jo about my phone call and our upcoming meeting, my sister said, "Roger Futrell said that adopted children have four parents." Technically true, but as I now take a seat on the couch next to my birth mother, I strongly believe it's preferable not to have all four of your parents in your life at once. Best go two at a time.

Mrs. Ballard—Mother? Orline?—I'm not sure what to call her—wants first to know about my children, her grandchildren. I tell her a little about Hollis and Tucker. Beyond curious, she wants to know more. I bring her up-to-date, going into some detail. She settles into the couch, folds her hands in her lap, her face bright and eager. She seems to want to fill in the gaps of time, to know as much about me and Betsy as I want to share. Then I ask her about her children—my siblings. She directs me to a wall along one side of the living room where I see a series of framed photographs, 12 in all, high school graduation photos of Larry, Bobby, Joe, Jimmy, Mimi, Sally, Orline, Ottie, Pattie, Susy, Dee, and Mary.

"There are 13 of you," Mrs. Ballard says. "You'll meet them all."

I wonder if, in fact, I have already met them, decades ago, playing baseball or swimming in the public pool. Given the small size of Bardstown, the approximation of Mrs. Ballard's house to my aunt and uncle's home, and the amount of time I spent here, I believe that I have, almost certainly. After a while, Sally directs us to the dining room where we sit down to a light lunch, followed by dessert.

"I could skip lunch and go right to dessert," my mother says.

I laugh. "I see where I got my sweet tooth," I say.

I don't stay too long, this first time. I hadn't planned on a long visit. I don't want to tax Mrs. Ballard physically, emotionally, and frankly, I wasn't sure what to expect. But now I know I will come back. Even more, Mrs. Ballard promises to include all my siblings in due course. I feel as if I have been given a priceless gift, the gift of a brand-new family.

As I hug my mother, she clings to me. Her breath comes quickly and I see that she's holding back tears. I keep my hand resting on her back, afraid to let go. Finally, she nods, I let go, and we walk to the door. Presuming she expects privacy and discretion about our relationship, I whisper, "Of course, this will be our secret."

"No secret, Tom," she says. "I'm 82 years old and I don't care who knows or what they think."

We hug once more and I kiss my mother goodbye.

I will come back a couple of weeks later and begin to meet my 12 siblings, the most wonderful, welcoming group of people I can ever imagine having as a family. They haven't known about me for half a century and now they can't do enough to take me in, to include me in their world, in their lives. When I consider my mother's family, all my cousins, and now all of my Bardstown biological brothers and sisters and *those* cousins, I realize that I have feet in two of the most prominent Catholic families in town. I count nearly 100 relatives, many I have yet to meet. I will return to Bardstown time and again, with Betsy, with Tucker, and with Mary Jo. I come for holidays, Sunday dinners, and I will drop in often, although, I admit, not often enough. I learn about George Gage, my biological father. He and Mrs. Ballard never married. He went off to war, fought and died in the Normandy Invasion in 1944.

At another family gathering, one of my sisters tells me that Orline's brother, my uncle Sam Simpson, rose to become a Master Distiller at Henry McKenna Distillery in Fairfield, Kentucky, and retired as Master Distiller at Barton Brands. Sam learned his trade from Coleman Bixler, his father-in-law, a fifth-generation distiller. Other family members worked at distilleries, and Coleman's brother Herman also became a Master Distiller. When I add in Augustus on my adopted family's side, it occurs to me that I have bourbon in my blood, everywhere I turn. It dawns on me, too, that Mrs. Ballard named me James Howard *Simpson*—her maiden name, and then after my uncle, the Master Distiller, the name I discovered on my birth certificate. All of this seems like something out of Charles Dickens, complete with this surprising twist at the end.

Life then intervenes, as some people say, an expression I hear too much and normally dismiss as a poor excuse. Life doesn't intervene. Life continues, inexorably, the good and the bad, and when you allow time to pass, you can never catch up. Time does pass, and I do wish I visit Mrs. Ballard—my birth mother—more frequently than I do. But soon 2004 rushes to its end, and then 2005 arrives with its own personal shock and awe, sneaking up on me out of nowhere, attacking me, knocking me flat on my ass, I struggle to visit my birth mother—I struggle, period—and then Christmas comes, and then New Year's 2005. By then it's too late to spend any more time.

"My prayer is for a good life and a good death," Mrs. Ballard tells me during one of my visits, words I love and will never forget.

To honor her request, my biological sister Mimi, a nun who has created a women's and children's hostel in Chile, is taking care of our mother when she passes.

"I made the decision not to submit her to the heroic horrors of modern medicine," Mimi says. "I have midwifed her into the afterlife."

My mother—Mrs. Orline Ballard—passes away, at home, in her living room, on New Year's Day, prayers answered.

No News Is Not Good News

(Things Are Just Getting Worse)

"It Was the Drugs, Tom"

LOOKING BACK, TRYING to grasp the sheer expanse of years I've lived—three-quarters of a century—blazing at me in mind-bending velocity of time, I consider a life played out in moments, all somehow neatly described in a series of three-word sentences, each one a screaming headline—

I'm a soldier.

I'm a lawyer.

I love you.

I'm making bourbon.

Seagram buys Bulleit.

Diageo buys Seagram.

I'm your mother.

… and …

I have cancer.

* * *

March 14, 2005.

I reach another birthday, no milestone, just a number, 62. I don't remember a celebration. I do remember complaining that I've become old. I insist on cake, not that I need an excuse for dessert, and request a trip to my favorite fast-food place—well, they're all my favorite—and order a birthday happy meal: burger, shake, double fries, pass the salt.

"You eat like a 16-year-old," Betsy says. "Sorry, that's not fair. A 12-year-old."

"Thanks," I say, swooping up a handful of fries, dredging them through a puddle of ketchup on my plate.

"That wasn't a compliment."

I grunt, nod, grin. Resigned to this life with me and to these occasionally infuriating moments, Betsy sighs, hugely whispers, "Happy Birthday," snags a dry fry, stuffs it in my mouth.

According to one doctor, eating this way has led to a recent bout with diverticulitis, a painful infection that feels like a heavyweight boxer repeatedly driving his fist into my lower intestines. For a short time, I vow to eat better, and I do, eating oatmeal and fruit and some other stuff I call health food, instead of my beloved fast-food diet. But as soon as the diverticulitis leaves and the pain in my lower half lessens, I return to my wanton eating ways. In fairness, my eating habits exist partly due to my life on the road. Except for an occasional business lunch or dinner at a high-end restaurant, I'm having it my way at Mickey D's or equivalent establishment.

As 2005 rolls in, Bulleit has begun to roll out, headed in the near future for all 50 states, a challenge and a triumph. In March, I spend a week in San Francisco performing Ambassadorship duties, visiting accounts, going on ride-alongs, pulling 16-hour days, and squeezing in time to hang out with Steve Beal and the 12 Apostles at Absinthe and other up-and-coming bars. At some point, after a large, late meal, I feel an excruciating pain in my left side, no doubt the diverticulitis returning for an encore. This time, though, the pain feels sharper and in a slightly different location. I tell Betsy about it during our nightly phone call. Concerned and vigilant, she phones Jim Borders, my internist, who says this calls for a colonoscopy, as soon as possible, "to rule out the worst-case stuff," the second-most-common phrase doctors learn in medical school after "take two of these and call me in the morning."

On April 27, back in Kentucky, I undergo a colonoscopy performed by Dr. Frank, a gentle, affable bear of a man with some resemblance to the comedian Jim Gaffigan. The procedure takes longer than expected, which Betsy, in the waiting room, takes as a sign of something—not right. Coming out of the anesthesia, and being told to get dressed and meet Dr. Frank in his office, I have a premonition. I don't know what to expect, but I do mumble a brief prayer as I button my shirt, "I promise to eat right, Lord, from now on, if anything should—"

I stop in mid-button, don't finish my prayer because I don't know what to ask for. I know only what I dread.

But it can't be, I think. *We're going into all 50 states. We're up to 30,000 cases, soon we'll hit 50,000. It's happening. Everything I'd worked for, dreamed about.*

Sitting across from Dr. Frank in his office, Betsy and I both lean forward in our chairs as he clears his throat, nods uncomfortably, and starts his first sentence with "Unfortunately."

I don't retain or comprehend much else of what he says, but I glimpse a string of words floating past, words and phrases I know I need to hear and absorb: "tumor"; "invading through muscularis mucosa into submucosal tissue focally"; "tumor"; "surgical intervention"; "actually right colon cancer, not left"; "colectomy"; *"tumor ... tumor ... tumor ..."*

I don't recall leaving Dr. Frank's office. I see us leaving the office area, passing people wearing white smocks, nurses in blue scrubs, receptionists directing us to another doctor, Dr. Atkins, at his office across town to schedule my upcoming colectomy, then everyone freezes in a kind of tableau, an incongruous Greek chorus, all wishing us good luck.

Good luck.

That is what the medical experts say I need, what I require.

Luck.

And that luck better be good.

"You have cancer," Betsy says, sitting in the driver's seat, hunched over the wheel, looking straight ahead, her voice shaking.

"Yeah," I say. "I heard. You want me to drive?"

"No, no, I'll drive." She fumbles with the keys. "We have to go to Dr. Atkins."

"First, we're going to McDonald's."

"What?"

"I'm starving."

"Tom, you have *cancer*."

"I know. But I have to eat. I'm craving some Chicken McNuggets and some fries. I'm dying for those fries."

Her mouth drops open.

"Sorry. Bad choice of words."

We opt for the drive-through and I devour a bag of McNuggets, fries, and a shake, eating off my lap while Betsy watches me in a daze, both horrified and amazed, and then we drive to Dr. Atkins's office. I remember nothing at all about this visit except standing unsteadily at reception on the way out and setting the date for my surgery, May 10, which leaves me time for a prescheduled business trip to New York. Nursing a food hangover from my feast at McDonald's and a drug hangover from the colonoscopy, feeling loopy and wasted, emotionally and physically, I literally stagger into the house. I step into the living room and a strange wave of nostalgia overcomes me. This house. This comfortable, stunning work of art, thanks completely to Betsy. She chose every piece of furniture and every accessory with such thoughtfulness, care, and quiet flair. I wander into the dining room, run my hand along the table, period English, then look at the chairs, antiques she found in Shelbyville, and the sideboard along the wall, filled with porcelain china, every item chosen or inherited, each one placed exactly.

I'll miss this house, I think.

I scan the room, my legs wobbly, my body weaving, my heart suddenly thumping.

No, I won't miss it. The dead don't miss anything. They're dead.

Will the neighbors miss me? Betsy will, my family will. But will my life make a dent in anyone else's psyche, minds, hearts? Does it matter?

I pull out a chair, sit heavily, lean my elbows onto the slick dining room table, and lower my head in my hands.

I have cancer.

I feel like a loser. A failure. I have let my family down. I have left so much unfinished. I have so much more to do. I have to get to *work*.

And then, as suddenly as the wave of emotion and despair and self-pity has rushed over me, I power through it all, somehow. I heave a sigh, and force myself to stand, and then walk out of the dining room.

Good luck.

I'll need more than that. I'll need strength and I'll need faith. And I'll need to fight.

*   *   *

In the beginning of May, Betsy and I arrive in New York for the official New York launch of Bulleit, a pre-operation whirlwind week of parties, interviews, promotions, and Happy Hours, culminating with the massive Derby Party at the Park Avenue Country Club. We hail a cab at LaGuardia and settle into the backseat for the rush-hour drive into Manhattan. I greet the cabdriver, dark-skinned, wearing a turban. Both of us chatty, interested in people, we begin a conversation. I identify Betsy and myself as born and bred Kentuckians. He tells us he is a Pakistani Muslim, living in Brooklyn, raising three daughters. We talk about the war in Iraq, express our concern, our sadness. We don't talk about politics. We talk about humanity—and the inhumanity of war.

"I lost a son," he says, quietly.

"No," I say. "I'm sorry."

"He died," the cabdriver says. "He was one year old."

Betsy gasps, grips my forearm.

"In the war ...," I say.

The cabdriver looks back at Betsy and me in the rearview mirror. I don't know if he can see Betsy's tears, but he nods, looks forward through the windshield, flicks at a tear sliding down his cheek, tightens his hands on the steering wheel.

"I have no words," I say, and then I repeat, "I'm so sorry."

"Death is not in my hand," he says. "Not in your hand. In no one's hand. Only in the hand of God."

Betsy grips my hand.

*   *   *

I don't think about the surgery. I *do* New York, 10 frenetic days, my hands first burning and then going numb from countless handshakes, the air in each room humming with optimism and promise, our previous six-year slow, deliberate pace a memory. We begin a new strategy, a rapid-fire approach, head-down, a sprint across the nation, fraught phrases appearing above me ricocheting all around me—"The launch, Tom, the launch"; "Fifty thousand cases this year, easy, Tom, easy"; "Whiskey-Fest in Chicago, a scene, Tom"; "Colorado loves you, Tom, loves you"; "*The Launch, Tom*"—and then the 10 days pass, and we're tucked into the backseat of another cab, heading out to LaGuardia for our Kentucky return, this cabdriver, serious, silent, a Manhattan to Long Island shortcut wizard, neither I nor Betsy in the mood to engage, all bantered-out.

At one point, the Manhattan skyline, our backdrop, receding, I say, not for the first time, "We should move to New York."

Betsy sniffs, resigned. I mention this pipedream of living in the city that never sleeps at least twice a year, usually when I'm wide awake in the middle of the night.

"We're from *Lexington*, Tom," she says, the subject closed.

"So, you're thinking about it," I say. "Good. Excellent. You don't have to give me your answer today. You can wait until after the surgery."

*   *   *

The chart reads, "A 62-year-old male with biopsy-proven colon cancer."

I have cancer.

And now I have it in writing.

I think about what's called *The Presumption*.

Everyone who has ever been in combat or diagnosed with cancer has it.

We carry with us the *presumption* that others will get hurt, and we won't.

Others will get cancer, and we won't.

We have to believe in The Presumption or nobody would ever enter the military.

But once you have cancer, you learn that The Presumption is just that.

*   *   *

May 10, 2005.

I have a blurry memory of being wheeled down a hallway, of muffled voices and laughter crackling above me in surround-sound, of the operating room's automatic doors whipping open, of feeling as if I'm watching myself on TV, the unfortunate patient in a doctor show drama, of those amplified sounds you hear, the bleating, beeping, buzzing, and then someone slips a plastic cone over my nose, tells me to breathe normally and count down from 100, which I do—99, 98, 90—and then all goes dark.

* * *

My mind drifting ...

At 23, a college grad, barely, I have enlisted. Now I am 24, a corpsman serving on the shores of Lake Michigan at Great Lakes Naval Hospital, Ward Three South. I witness those who have left the killing fields and have entered into hell.

The wounded arrive directly from the war. Transport vehicles disgorge a flow of gurneys containing maimed men still in their muddy and bloody fatigues. A few soldiers have Purple Hearts pinned to their shredded jackets. This world I walk through, attending these torn bodies and terrified young men, removes all color from my vision. Everything goes completely black and white ... and red. I walk among rows of amputees. I pass men with holes in their bodies so deep you can see all the way through them. We change dressings, peel off bandages once white now bubbling scarlet, apply new gauze, wait an hour or two, repeat. We do what we can, but there is so little we can do. We wish we could force the powers that be to walk side-by-side with us in this place and see this carnage up close, this American carnage, the result of their decisions made impersonally, in the comfort and safety and anonymity of some secluded closed-door haven in the American capitol. Maybe if they saw this, they would find another way to settle disputes. The men I treat are heroes, every one of them, but not one of them wanted to become a hero this way.

And drifting back ... I suddenly feel sick to my stomach.

A pain, flesh tearing, chews into my right side.

I'm thirsty and my vision goes gray, cloudy. I blink toward the ceiling and I realize I am not in Three South, I am not 24, I'm 62, I'm here, in Lexington, at Saint Joseph Hospital, my mouth so dry, my arms strait-jacketed to my sides, attached to machines, an IV—I'm so *thirsty*—and, yes, I remember it all, the whirlwind days in New York, the launch, the handshakes, the promise of the future, and now the hole I have in my side, swathed in bandages, and the throbbing neon realization pulsing before my eyes—I have cancer.

Dear God, help me beat this.

I've been in a foxhole and in a cancer ward, and I have not met an atheist either place.

*   *   *

Two days gone. I drift in and out of sleep. Barely awake, I scan my body and see flesh attached to tubes, wires, electronics. A monitor with green lines dancing. Draining tubes connected to my stomach. IV stabbed into my forearm. Catheter. At unpredictable intervals alarms honk, summoning nurses to switch out cellophane bags of fluids, painkillers. The nurses float by, hover, poke, prod, insert my middle finger into a contraption that records my oxygen levels, jab my arm to remove my blood. Invariably they arrive 30 seconds after I've fallen asleep, jar me awake bleary-eyed, semi-conscious. They have terrible timing. They can't help it. I know them. I have been one of them. I know the rhythm of their job and I know that they are doing it well.

*   *   *

Day two, I'm awake, my vision foggy, the pain boring into my side. I blink like a madman and see Dr. Atkins standing stoically at my bedside.

"The pain," I mutter.

"This line," he says, pointing at a tube leading somewhere. "For morphine. You press this button."

He holds his hand above a button that looks like a doorbell.

"What if I hold it down too long? Will I overdose?"

Interesting. Along with cancer comes paranoia.

"It's on a governor, Tom. It's regulated."

"I could hit it twice," I say. "Or three times. I could press it down, lean on it, never let it go—"

"You know what? Let's have the nurse administer the morphine for you today. We'll revisit self-administration tomorrow. Sound good?"

I fall back asleep.

Maybe Dr. Atkins never came by. Maybe I dream that.

*   *   *

Day … three? I don't know. I have lost time. I have lost days. My throat remains as dry as a sand trap. I'm so thirsty, I can't drink enough. I swig water, crave tea, then one day, I go off clear liquids and sip some milk. Bad idea. My insides clench, I throw up, my stomach wracked, twisted. I nearly strangle myself in a tangle of tubes and wires.

Then one day—day four, maybe—Dr. Atkins announces that I'm recovering nicely. I blink again like a madman, wondering if he's wandered into the wrong room. He disappears as if into a mist, and eventually a team of nurses arrive, unplug tubes, disconnect wires, remove the catheter, and a guy in a blue smock and a hairnet appears with a tray and serves me a scrumptious meal consisting of something brown and something green that jiggles. I glance at a menu tucked under the green jiggly thing, confirm my room number, and read "Semisolid food." I might agree about "semisolid," might seek a second opinion about the term "food." An hour or two later, Dr. Atkins returns for a cameo appearance and says, "Okay, Tom, up. You need to get up and walk."

I start to sit up. My head swims, I slide backward, nearly black out. Later, determined and finding a reservoir of strength, I try again. This time, I sit up, fight through a wave of dizziness and nausea, inhale, and, guided by a new tag-team of nurses, ease out of the bed. I take a few steps, pull up, stop, decide I've had enough and double back. The nurses cheer like I've crossed the finish line at the Boston Marathon.

Later that day, more nurses arrive and I try again. Flanked by two of the more solid among them, field hockey fullbacks in another life, I make it out of the room and venture into the hall.

"What's that, about 15 feet?" I mumble.

"At least," one says.

"Don't forget to add the way back," the other says. "Now you're up to 30."

"Tomorrow morning you'll go even farther," the first nurse says.

"Promise?"

"Yes, sir, I'm gonna make you."

"I'm holding you to that," I say.

The next day I make it into the hall, all the way past the next room, 20 feet, and back, then on my next trip, I go 25 feet out and back, and the morning of the next day, I make it all the way to the nurses' station.

"How you all doing?" I say.

Words of encouragement, cheering.

"You're doing *great*," a nurse says.

"Well, thanks, and you better keep an eye on me, or I might just escape, sprint right out of here."

They laugh, all of them. I join them, despite a gurgle and a dull pain in my stomach. Then, in love with these nurses, I turn around and head back to my room, feeling as if I've just walked 10 miles.

That night I entertain visitors, a montage of faces, edging up to the bed—Betsy, Mary Jo, Ronnie, Tucker, Hollis, Kathy, George, and a few other close friends, my support team. In truth, I don't really *entertain* them. Unless their idea of a good time is looking at a 62-year-old lawyer, Founder and Ambassador of Bourbon, lying withered and wasted in a hospital bed on a cancer ward.

Day six, we leave. I sign some papers, thank God for Betsy's Hilliard-Lyons insurance, bid a fond farewell to my IV pole, my dancing partner, and wait for the discharge nurse to plunk me down on a wheelchair and wheel me out of here. At home, finally, always the good soldier, I obey my doctor's orders—take regular, slow walks and the rest of the time, take it easy. I take slow walks. Half-block walks, around the block once, then twice. A regimen I will ultimately rewind and repeat that year. At night, I try to sleep and can't. Pain shooting down my side and into my lower back, I stand at my bedside because I can't find any comfort lying in bed.

"This is what they call being in 'stable condition'?" I grumble to Betsy.

"You're not out of the woods yet, Tom," Betsy says.

"I don't even see the forest," I say, grumbling, now my default setting.

* * *

"Mr. Bulleit is an extremely pleasant 62-year-old gentleman whom I met briefly during his hospital stay at St. Joseph. He comes today for evaluation and treatment plan regarding a stage III colon cancer."

I sit with my oncologist, Dr. Monty S. Metcalfe, the author of that opinion, which I read in his hospital report. Betsy sits next to me. She reaches over and squeezes my hand. Her face has gone ash-white, her expression dark. I look past Monty at the diplomas mounted on the wall behind him in his office. He has more than a few. I face the diplomas because I need to process what he has just said. Monty has ordered 18 sessions of chemotherapy. My protocol. I am to start right away. The number 18 hangs over the three of us. A daunting number. A whale of a number. For the moment, we all smile pleasantly, taking it in. We are all pleasant people, I, being extremely pleasant.

"What's the chance of a cure?"

Betsy, I think, asks this, or maybe I do in my very offhand, distracted, pleasant way.

Monty shifts in his chair. "Fifty percent. We can up that to 75, with chemotherapy, depending ..."

His voice shuts off. I wait for him to complete his sentence. He doesn't appear inclined to, so I urge him to keep going, to give me the bad news, well, to tell me the truth.

"Depending on ...?" I say, prompting him.

"How the chemotherapy goes," he says.

"Eighteen sessions," Betsy says. "That seems like a lot."

"Normal for this cancer," Monty says. "Three cycles of six treatments per cycle, one per week, with two weeks between cycles. So, that would be 22 weeks all told, about five months. Should be completed by Christmas."

Betsy and I go silent, and then Monty says, "Yeah, it is a lot."

"Merry Christmas," I say.

More silence.

"Well, okay," I say, and I clap my hands, startling Betsy and Monty. "Let's get to it. I have work to do."

"See, that's why I'm confident that you will do well," Monty says. "People who have had good luck in their business, successful people, generally do well."

"Why is that?" I ask.

"They tend to be optimists," Monty says, and then, smiling, says, "They believe they're going to live. They are determined."

"I have a lot more work to do," I say. "I'm actually just getting started."

"Unfinished business," Betsy says, gripping my hand, looking at me, looking into me, and then she turns away, and looks past Monty, lasering into the diplomas on his wall, looking for solace, looking for hope, screaming without speaking.

* * *

Rummaging through my dresser drawer, tucked in the back, co-mingled with my dog tags, I find what I'm looking for.

My Saint Christopher medal.

Actually, *our* Saint Christopher medal, shared with my father. He wore it in World War II and handed it off to me before I left for Vietnam. Saint Christopher, the patron saint of travelers, looked over us both in our respective wars. Travelers, we came back alive, subjects of and recipients of my mother's continual prayers. I pull the Saint Christopher medal out of the dresser drawer and press it against my chest. I sway slightly, close my eyes, and say, "Bring me home ... to ..."

I swallow and whisper, "Just, please, bring me home."

* * *

I think about dying. I think about leaving this life too soon. The thought annoys me. I can't die. I want to outlive all the shit-birds I've met who've tainted my life. I've tried consciously to remove them from my daily existence and have for the most part succeeded. But still, knowing that I'll be dead and they won't be, that they will have outlived me, bothers the hell out of me. Outliving the shit-birds may not be the grandest or most inspirational motivation, but if it gets me through the chemo and kills this cancer, I'll take it. Hell, I'll take anything. And, seriously, I do want to outlive the shit-birds.

* * *

Six weeks after my operation, on July 1, 2005, chemotherapy begins. Pathologically early, I arrive 20 minutes before 11:00, my scheduled time. I plunk down in the waiting room on a loveseat next to Betsy, get absorbed in the latest *Road and Track*, picture myself behind the wheel of some souped-up, muscle-bound Porsche, driving 140 miles per hour out of here. Shortly, a courteous nurse interrupts my daydream, I fill out some paperwork, sign a few forms, pay the co-pay, and Betsy and I follow her down a hallway with colorful art on the walls, into an open area with some beds and people hooked up to IVs, most of them zonked, and then into a private room with a cushy chair for Betsy and a recliner for me. The nurse inserts the IV lead into my new built-in dual lumen porto-a-cath, then doses me with Leucovorin, used to prevent the chemo drug from seriously messing me up, and then attaches a plastic bag of the chemo itself, and after my system kicks in, the chemo—installment one—begins to surge through my bloodstream. In this incongruous setting, our new normal, Betsy and I struggle to find our comfort levels. Overachievers, both, we need tasks. We arrange ourselves in silence. She settles in, reads a book, and I, never one to relax, even during chemotherapy, work. I jot notes for the upcoming launch of Bulleit Bourbon in Connecticut. I have a plan, a mission—keep working and stay ahead of the cancer. I'll fly to Hartford on July 6, work the market, returning to Lexington two days later for chemotherapy round two. I also start preparing for a good-natured scotch versus bourbon debate in a month or so—in front of an audience, I'll take on Evan Cattanach, a dear friend, an ambassador for scotch—set for the Diageo Reserve Brand Summit in San Francisco at the Four Seasons. I want to take a few days in San Francisco this time, see as many of the 12 Apostles as Steve Beal can convene, and then spend a night or two with Betsy at the stunning Auberge du Soleil in Napa. I am determined not to allow this cancer to interfere with my life. I will keep it at bay. I consider it a distraction. A temporary detour. I will fight it. I will keep myself on the road, moving forward.

That's the pep talk I give myself in this recliner as the chemo causes me to close my eyes and I begin to nod off. *The cancer can't beat you*, I say, darkness coming in. *You can only beat yourself ...*

I tolerate the first treatment fairly well, make it to Hartford, participate in the launch, and get through the socializing, feeling fatigued, subdued. I return to Lexington, muttering my mantra: one down, 17 to go.

Chemotherapy session number two arrives sooner than I expect and this time, settling into my recliner, watching the infusion nurse insert the IV line into my port-a-cath, I feel tired, weak, and a little sick to my stomach. I don't write notes or read much during this session. I just sit, reflect, and plan, trying to prepare for the San Francisco summit. Lying back, pulling the blanket up to my neck, I hear voices outside my room. A woman speaks to someone about arranging for hospice care for her father. Hospice care? Isn't that when you're at the *end*? I know it's irrational to take this overheard conversation personally, but I want to interrupt and shout, *"It's too soon."* Suddenly, I begin to float away, fighting off sleep pathetically as I acknowledge that, yes, chemotherapy round two is slightly kicking my ass.

*　*　*

After round two, people talk to me philosophically about chemotherapy—well-meaning friends and family, either with firsthand knowledge or having been caretakers—all of them issuing a warning. They want me to understand that the effect of chemotherapy is cumulative.

"It's the third day after that gets you," a friend says.

"They call it the third day chemo flu," someone else says.

I call Dr. Metcalfe. He confirms what everyone has told me. Watch out for the third day chemo flu.

"Is there a medical term for that?" I ask him.

"Yes, we call it the third day chemo flu," he says.

On Friday, July 15, after chemotherapy session three, I prepare for the third day flu to hit. I don't believe it will. I feel immune to such things. Pumped up by the Leucovorin, I go to bed feeling high, energized, and, surprisingly, smarter.

I barely wake up Saturday. I feel pummeled. I drag through the day in slow motion. Sunday, I feel improved, on the mend. *I'm different*, I think. *I'm tougher. I will not experience the typical chemotherapy fallout. I'm not going to get the third day chemo flu.*

I'm so right. Monday morning, I wake up refreshed. I work out, spend a couple hours reading, writing, and speak to my friend, Jack Russell.

"Tom," he says, "I know you feel like you'll never be strong again, but you will."

That one thought fills me up. I file it away, calling on Jack's reminder at the times I feel my weakest.

Then I meet my friend Bo Fugazzi for an early lunch. I get back about 1:30, step inside the house, and—wham—a devastating, overwhelming fatigue drops onto my shoulders like a 500-pound weight. I take one step and stagger. I literally cannot walk. I somehow manage to inch my way into the bedroom and collapse onto the bed.

"Mondays," I mutter into my pillow. "Third day chemo flu. Okay, you got me. I might have to lose Mondays."

I don't get out of bed until Wednesday.

Wednesday morning, I call Dr. Metcalfe. He prescribes a heavy dose of iron pills. I down those and by Thursday mid-afternoon, debilitating fatigue, stomach cramps, and diarrhea attack me. The plague of third day chemo flu has arrived in full force and has knocked me to my knees. Thursday night, six days into my third-day chemo flu, I stare at my alarm clock by my bedside, and as if coming out of a trance, realize that Betsy is out of town, at a conference. I will have to drive myself to chemotherapy session number four.

"Not a problem," I say, right before I drag myself out of bed and sprint into the bathroom, stabbing pain driving through my stomach as I run.

I make it to chemotherapy session four, driving myself. On the way, I think about Betsy's mom, Rosemary Brooks, an inspiring force of nature. Mrs. Brooks became a feminist long before someone coined the term. Someone once asked her, "What factor played a role in the rise of feminism?"

"The electric starter on an automobile," Mrs. Brooks said. "Before the electric starter you had to drive from man to man because a man had to crank the engine. The electric starter changed all that."

Never thought of that. Few people have.

Later in life, when Mrs. Brooks was diagnosed with cancer, she drove herself to 42 radiation treatments.

I believe I can drive myself to one.

* * *

Before my session, I have an appointment with Dr. Metcalfe, who prescribes medication to settle the diarrhea caused by the mix of iron pills and chemo. I'll discover that these pills won't work. He'll prescribe a stronger anti-diarrhea medication. When those fail, he'll go to even stronger pills.

I endure chemo session four, feeling shockingly upbeat. Driving home, boosted by the Leucovorin, I feel buoyed, stronger. A false high, I know, but I decide to take advantage of it. I stop by Christ the King Church, ease into a pew near the back, fold my hands, bow my head, and mutter a prayer of thanks. That's it. That's all I can come up with. I can't pray for anything else. I don't have it in me. The act of asking makes me feel too egotistical, too selfish, too proud. *I need to give to get*, I think. *What have I given? Is love enough?* I love my family, I love those who surround me, who support me in every way—friends, business associates, my co-workers. I have been blessed to have all these people in my life, so I just say, aloud, to God, "Thank You for Your love." I wait 30 seconds or so, then pick myself up and leave the church. In the car, driving home, I ask myself, *What the hell is wrong with you? What were you doing in there? You should have prayed to beat this CANCER.*

Didn't it occur to me.

Well, it did, of course.

I guess I thought I'd be asking God for too much.

That night, Friday, and Saturday morning, I feel a shade short of outstanding, once again chalking that up to the Leucovorin. Then Saturday afternoon, just before 3:00, my entire body, with the speed of a missile, descends into hell. I get the daily double of stomach cramps and diarrhea, then a savage pain slices down my back, and finally a wave of fatigue so intense I can barely lift the water glass on my nightstand. After my third or fourth trip to the bathroom, I fall onto the bed, my heart pounding, my breath coming in staccato bursts, in gasps. For the first time since I started chemotherapy, I feel physically ravaged and I feel—scared.

Fear.

I don't remember feeling fear before, not even in Vietnam.

But now, crawling back into the bathroom, my stomach contorted into knots of agony, my mind racing, reeling, I feel deathly scared. I peer into the darkness and I see no light at the end of the tunnel. But what scares me to death is that I don't even see the tunnel.

Betsy flies home early from her conference. I'm thankful she's here, but I can't relay that to her because I'm so weak I can barely acknowledge her presence. I spend every waking minute of the next five days in the bathroom with diarrhea, bloated, doubled over, hallucinating from a high fever.

On Friday, Dr. Metcalfe deduces that in addition to experiencing extreme toxicity from the Leucovorin, I have developed an ileum, a collapsed colon. He orders me straight to Saint Joseph's Hospital. I do not pass go; I do not go through admitting. I am taken immediately upstairs, floor six, to a hospital bed in my old haunt on the oncology ward. My chart sums it up:

"... he received his fourth week of treatment last Friday and after that began to develop progressive problems with increasing diarrhea, increasing anorexia.... The patient is a very pleasant, 62-year-old gentleman who is admitted today because of complications related to his ongoing chemotherapy."

There it is. In black and white. Right in Dr. Metcalfe's notes.

The solution to my problem.

I'm too damn pleasant.

* * *

The nurses swarm, insert an IV, a PICC line, a catheter, an access port, and an NG tube from my throat to my stomach. They draw blood, plug me into monitors, hand me the doorbell end of a clothesline cord to press for morphine. Consulting doctors arrive, consult, specify, confirm. I have an ileus, a paralysis of the intestines—the colon, in my case—blocking my intestinal tract. And, blood work shows a C-Diff infection, a severe infection of the colon. Great. Bacteria has mounted a savage attack on whatever's left of my thread-bare colon. I receive drugs to fight the infection and I am to eat nothing by mouth. Food will enter through the PICC line. I'm so thirsty I ache. At one point—the days all swim into one long, continuous, unending blurry day—I see a nurse standing over me, adjusting or inserting yet another tube, 50 cc's of ice per hour.

"I have a Porsche down the street," I mumble to her. "I'll give it to you for a Diet Coke."

"I don't drive a stick," she says.

Either taking pity on me or I'm so up the creek that it doesn't matter, the nurse returns with early ice chips and allows me a solitary drip every hour. Then hiccups for a week, jacking the NG tube up and down my throat with each.

* * *

Eight days later, my closely cropped beard grown out into an unruly Grizzly Adams bush, a throbbing fever blister exploding over my entire lower lips, giving the impression that I've grown a third lip, my body pale as a corpse, emaciated, having lost 15 pounds, my eyes dark, ringed, hollow, I sit slumped in the chair next to my hospital bed and methodically bathe myself with cotton swabs and a damp washcloth. Somehow, I have wriggled through this ordeal and come out alive. I feel like a survivor of a brutal and terrible war—decimated, dazed, bloodied, but *alive*. Later, after my refreshing sponge bath, I shuffle down the hall, leading my IV tube contraption, my companion, an extension of myself, and enter a room bathed in dim green light for my cancer rehabilitation session.

I was probably getting ahead of myself, allowed my optimism to intrude, I think. *This is cancer. It kicks your ass, hard. That's why the word "cancer" has become one of the most frightening words in our vocabulary.*

That evening, drifting in and out of sleep, I became marginally aware of a noise in my room. The sound of movement, of feet shuffling. Then someone clears his throat and softly calls my name. I blink my eyes open and see Father Frank, our parish priest, standing at the foot of my bed. He smiles kindly.

"What is this?" I say, groggily, and then I sit up, trying to focus on Father Frank's face, and I say, "Are you—is it that bad—why are you here?"

"How are you doing, Tom?" Father Frank says, his voice gentle, soothing.

"I don't know. How am I doing?"

My vision begins to clear and I see that he holds a sacrament book and cradles his kit against his side. He smiles again, and takes his vestment out of the kit.

"Are you giving me Last Rites?" I say, jolted awake. "Father Frank, seriously, is this *it?*"

"Oh, no, no, it's not what you think."

"It's not?"

"No. You can give Last Rites for the sick as well as for the dying."

"Which is it?"

"Actually, Tom, Last Rites started as a ritual for the sick."

"That's great. Why don't I feel better?"

Father Frank grins, "You're not dying, Tom."

"I feel like I could die," I say. "Pretty much any minute."

"Well, you're not. I am going to perform Last Rites, which we call, in your case, Anointment of the Sick."

He reads the prayers, sprinkles Holy Water over my body, recites the Ritual in his low, clerical baritone, places a cross with oil on my forehead, nods, and we both say, "Amen."

"Excuse me."

I squint and see Colby Atkins, my surgeon, standing in the doorway. He clasps my chart to his chest. He looks from Father Frank to me, then back to Father Frank, stunned.

"Nobody called me. They should've contacted me first, calling the priest for Last Rites—"

"Oh, no, I'm giving Last Rites for the sick."

"You can do that?"

Now I look from Father Frank to Dr. Atkins. "I got the priest, I got the doctor—somebody tell me if I'm coming or going."

"I'll leave you to it," Dr. Atkins says, backing out of the room, relieved.

* * *

Then, miraculously, I complete what I would call a Hail Mary pass and begin a comeback, slowly, stealthily, oblivious to the passage of time. At some point, I graduate to a diet of clear liquids, then to light, solid foods. That green jiggly substance that approximated food at my previous hospital stay returns to my tray accompanied by something gray that oozes. I take a spoonful of each and determine that if the cancer doesn't kill me, this will. I decide to stick with liquids until I can at least identify the food the hospital staff serves me. Another day or so passes, and a nurse appears with a razor and a can of shaving cream. I make my way into the bathroom and, gratefully, I shave. In the mirror, a sunken face the color of paper stares back at me. Another day dissolves, and so-called food appears on my tray. I eat whatever the smock-wearing dietician puts in front of me—green stuff that may be mashed peas, orange stuff that may be mashed carrots, brown stuff that may be chocolate pudding. I scarf it all down as if I'm eating bags of Chicken McNuggets from McDonald's. After a day of gorging on solid food, I feel stronger, and then one day, to confirm this, a pit crew of nurses converges on me and removes my PICC line, most of the tubes, and unplugs me from the monitor. The spokesperson, a thin, energetic woman with intelligent eyes, confirms that I have turned a corner, but I'm still not out of the woods, an impressive description of my condition captured in two common clichés. She's right. I continue to run a low-grade temperature and begin to experience cabin fever. Additionally, I toss and turn all night, fighting night sweats and violent attacks of hiccups. But painstakingly slowly, a familiar feeling returns. I begin to feel—human.

One night, unable to sleep, staring at a vague pattern in the ceiling resembling Abraham Lincoln's profile, then glancing at the time on the digital clock by the bed—3:44 a.m.—I decide to plan my funeral.

I start to create a guest list, culling through names and faces all the way back to my childhood, quickly abandon that idea, relinquishing the responsibility of who should attend to Betsy. I'll be dead and won't care and, even better, I won't have to mingle. She can invite anyone she wants, except for those shit-birds whose funerals I really need to attend first. I consider then who should give the eulogy and whom I should entrust to present a fond memory or two about me. My life's highlights. The summary of a life in five minutes, max. What's the opposite of a lifetime? A deathtime? I maintain that no speech will extend past five minutes. So who should speak? Easy. My nephew, Dr. Rosario Picardo, minister and author. I call him "The Bishop."

I also want a military element. I feel certain about that. Most of all, I want music. That's really what matters most, the music. I should put my musical selections in writing, attach them to my will. I'll do that as soon as I can sit up and write without feeling the need to run to the bathroom.

As for my musical selections, I would lead off with "The Battle Hymn of the Republic" for Dad, and George, my two fathers, and for me, and to honor those who died in the red snow of Belgium and the bloody brown dirt of I Corps. I want the song sung a cappella by a Marine in full dress blues. After that, I want "I Will Find You" from the movie *Last of the Mohicans*. I love that song for its haunting beauty and because it moves me to *act*, to find you, as the song says, to find what I need to do. The song motivates me. Then "Don't Cry for Me, Argentina" from *Evita*, another stirring song about getting what you want and what you deserve, and leaving it at that. Next, I'll go to the Sarah Brightman and Andrea Bocelli duet, "Time to Say Goodbye," which brings me to tears every time I hear it. Then I'll segue to another military song, "Brandywine," the 7th Cavalry charge, played cheerfully as the cavalry rode to Little Big Horn, the soldiers blindly confident and numbingly unaware as they headed to their slaughter. Strangely, I find the song uplifting, a necessary mood choice for my funeral. Next, "Storms Never Last," by Jessie Colter, a semi-duet with her husband, Waylon Jennings, a profound message in those lyrics, a sentiment by which I live my life, or, in this case, *lived* my life. Then I'll go to "Knockin' on Heaven's Door" by Guns N' Roses, even now imagining Slash's opening guitar solo gives me chills. I'll follow that with two celestial voices, Tina Turner, growling and wailing "River Deep, Mountain High," surrounded by Phil Spector's Wall of Sound, and then the immortal Otis Redding singing "I've Been Loving You Too Long" from deep in his soul. I'll end with Southern Gospel, Jamie Wilson and her band singing "Ain't No Grave Gonna Hold My Body Down," the punctuation to a life well-lived, finally shutting it down.

Yes, I want a small funeral, in a church, wall-to-wall music, a few moments of memories, maybe have someone mention what I want engraved on my headstone—"Husband, Father, HM3 Bulleit." Then, done, the mourners will file out, convene in the social hall, raise a glass, drink some Bulleit Bourbon, and call it a night, call it a life, call it closing time. Now, let's move on. That's what we do. We push forward, we move on. Last call. Close the bar. Closing. Time.

* * *

I must drift off to sleep because I don't hear Dr. Metcalfe coming into my room, but when I open my eyes, I see him standing next to me, a wide smile stretched across his face.

"Well, Tom, you gave us a scare, and as always, I've enjoyed being with you, but we've come to that time."

"That *time*," I say, coming out of a fog, the words *Closing Time* flashing like a broken neon sign in my brain. "You mean—"

"Yes. I'm writing a discharge order."

I sit up. "I'm going home?"

"As soon as the nurse flushes and removes the IV, you're out of here."

"Shock probation," I mutter.

Monty tilts his head. "I'm not sure I know what that is."

"You get handed a prison sentence, and then for some reason the judge suspends it, puts you on probation."

"Lawyers," he says, shaking his head, but more a gesture of respect than disapproval. That's how I take it, anyway.

"I couldn't have said it better," he says.

"I'm in shock and I'm on probation," I say.

"We will be seeing each other soon. When you get your strength back, we have to resume the chemotherapy. We will be lowering the dose. Hopefully, that will prove more tolerable."

I want to correct him, ask, *What do you mean "we,"* but I just murmur, "Oh, I'm looking forward to it."

* * *

Later, as Betsy and I pack up our stuff, I do a quick calculation. "Thirteen days in the hospital, is that right?"

"Counting the first night, two weeks, Tom."

"It's like I closed my eyes for a minute and when I woke up, two weeks had gone by." I look at her. "I haven't missed two days of work in my life, never mind two weeks."

"You haven't had cancer before, either."

I stop packing my bag, peer out the window. "I can't remember who told me this, maybe Monty, I don't remember—"

I squint, keep looking out the window, and then I go quiet.

"What?" Betsy says, coming up behind me, gently rubbing my back.

"They said, 'Tom, you're either going to die or you won't. You will or you won't. You don't have much say about that. But it would really help if you worked. Don't sit at home and feel sorry for yourself.'"

I look at Betsy, and I see—

A single working mother with a dying husband.

This ordeal is far harder for her.

It's easier to go than to wait.

* * *

I arrive home, tipping the scales, officially, at 128 pounds. I am in shock. I have weighed 148 pounds, give or take a pound, for decades. I last weighed 128 pounds, exactly, when I returned from Vietnam 36 years ago. But at that time, at that weight, I was 128 pounds of muscle, lean, wiry, and fit, the strongest I have ever been in my life. Now, at that same 128 pounds, I am the *weakest* I have ever been in my life. I come into our living room from the car, feeling out of breath, as if I have just run 10 miles, when I have only walked 10 yards from our driveway. I sigh heavily and face the stairs leading up to our bedroom. I exhale and reach for the railing. I feel frail and frozen and old. And I feel sick. My ambition drives me. *I need to go back to work.* I take a deep breath, grab the railing with every ounce of my strength, and haul myself up to the first stair. I plant myself there after the six-inch climb, and I pause, exhausted. I shake my head and laugh at the sheer ridiculousness of this. I have to laugh or I will scream. I exhale, grunt, and pull myself up to the second step. I have, what, 15 more steps to climb? I crane my neck toward the landing above as if it's the peak of Mount Everest. It looks so far away. The climb looks impossible. I'm suddenly so fatigued that I want to sit down, but I force myself to go up to the third stair … and then the fourth. I keep going, hauling myself up each stair by pulling on the railing. I make it halfway up the stairs, to the eighth stair … the ninth … one more stair … one more …

I lose count of the stairs and I lose track of time. But I don't stop. I *will* myself up each stair. It takes me five minutes to make it to the second floor, or maybe it takes an hour. I have no idea. Finally, I arrive at the second-floor landing. I want to shout and raise my arms in triumph, but I seriously have to go to the bathroom, my reward for making it here, and then, moments later, I emerge from the bathroom, slumped over, destroyed, and I shuffle to the bedroom, and dive bomb onto the bed, Martin Luther King, Jr.'s words ringing in my head—"Every journey starts with a single step," and I think, *that includes this one, the journey up my stairs, into the bathroom, into the bedroom, and eventually downstairs, outside, down the driveway, down the block, and back to work, back to my life.*

* * *

I set goals. Today I will attempt to take a shower. That single activity involves a series of brutally exhausting actions—walking into the bathroom, getting undressed, turning on the shower, soaping my body, shampooing my hair, turning off the shower, toweling off, getting dressed, walking back into the bedroom. This all demands laser focus and nearly superhuman physical exertion. I promise myself that I will never again take the simple act of showering for granted.

Having conquered showering, I add a new goal the next day, something more daunting. I plan to walk downstairs and go into the kitchen. If that goes well, the next day, I will go downstairs, enter the kitchen, and then walk the downstairs perimeter. The next day, I will walk downstairs, go into the kitchen, walk the downstairs perimeter, go outside, walk to the end of the driveway, and then do everything in reverse. I imagine myself walking around the block, but I put that goal, conservatively, at a week away.

I hear a familiar sound outside, a rhythmic whap-whap-whap coming from the backyard. I look through our bedroom window and see Tucker outside dribbling his basketball and shooting at our backyard hoop. I watch my 13-year-old son and feel a wave of sadness, followed by impotence. I'm a failure. I should be out there with him, with my boy, shooting hoops, horsing around, being his *dad*, but I can't. I physically can't. The cancer has cut away my manhood, my strength, and now this disease has ripped out my fatherhood.

Stop feeling sorry for yourself, Tom.

I hear those words. But I haven't spoken them. They come from a different voice.

My father, who lost an eye in the Battle of the Bulge and who lived with shrapnel lodged in his body, who lived with pain, and disappointment, and frustration, and yet never complained. At least not aloud. At least not to me.

Lose the self-pity, Tom.

Walk around the block. And tomorrow, do it again, only walk longer, walk a block and a half, and the next day, walk two blocks.

Whap, whap, whap.

I watch Tucker dribble the basketball and then I watch him launch a shot.

Swish.

I'll be out there with him soon, I promise myself.

I head down the stairs, walking gingerly, purposefully, and then I slowly walk down the block. The next day, I walk down the block once, continue halfway, and then double back. The next day, I walk down the block twice.

This third day, another voice comes into my head, a distinctive voice I've heard over the years on newsreels and in television footage of World War II. The voice speaks with authority, beseeching me with a message I hear to this day, words I live by.

"Success is not final. Failure is not fatal; it is the courage to continue that counts."

Words spoken by Winston Churchill.

* * *

Walking around the block becomes my job—temporary (hopefully) and poor paying but highly incentivized. I put myself on a schedule. I walk around the block twice, morning and afternoon, then I increase to three times around the block twice a day, then go to four times around the block twice a day. I push myself to my limit, but I don't push myself *past* my limit. Another life rule I follow religiously: *Do what you can, just don't do less.*

One morning, I slowly negotiate down the stairs, answering the front doorbell to sign for a package. I carry a nondescript, thin FedEx box with a Diageo return address into the dining room, place it on the table, and carefully open the package. Gene, our Brand Manager, has sent me a "Last of the Great Bourbons" poster signed by my co-workers at Diageo, everyone who attended the Diageo Reserve Brand Summit in San Francisco, the event I missed because I lay near death in the St. Joseph's Hospital cancer ward. On the poster, below a giant bottle of Bulleit Bourbon, sits a swell of signatures, an overwhelming number of names. More than 100 people have autographed the poster. Below the names, someone has written: "Get well soon, Tom."

The poster, the signatures, the sentiment deeply touch me—and motivate me.

Yes, I really do have to get back to my job, the fulltime one that actually pays me.

* * *

I begin the long trip back. I don't make the trip alone. I'm supported on each side, all sides, every day, by Betsy, of course, my children, my friends, Mary Jo and Ronnie, and our Bardstown family. They all visit me frequently at home, and, as I find out, they came to the hospital as well, although I don't remember, my mind turned to mush during those two weeks, a virtual blank. A week passes, then another, and a third, and gradually I put back some weight and start to regain my strength. Looming before me I see scribbled on my calendar my return to chemotherapy in late August. I had originally penciled in 14 sessions remaining. *Fourteen* more sessions. A ridiculous number. A daunting number. A deflating number. A necessary number. I will need every ounce of my strength.

The night before I return to chemotherapy, I attend a charity cocktail party hosted by Colonel Ted Bassett, a friend and former Marine who all but created Keeneland Race Course in Lexington, inarguably the country's most beautiful racetrack. At the party, Colonel Bassett, bourbon in hand, corners me. He slaps me on the back, hard enough to knock the wind out of me, and keeps his hand resting on my shoulder.

"Glad to see you, Tom," he says.

"Thank you, Colonel. I'm glad I'm here."

"It's wonderful. Now get back on the horse."

"Yes, sir," I say, a corporal in the presence of a colonel, stifling an urge to salute.

* * *

Back on the horse.

I return to St. Joseph's to continue chemotherapy, at 50 percent of my original dose, Monty assuring me that the adjustment will make very little, if any difference. I sit with Betsy who leaves after an hour, after I've been stabbed with my IV and nestled into my familiar recliner with a blanket tucked up to my throat. She returns with our chemotherapy lunch—my lucky lunch, I hope—McDonald's Chicken McNuggets, fries, and a shake.

I sit, munching the chicken nuggets, aware that I'm currently enjoying the fun part of the process, the real test coming in a couple of days at home when I will find out whether I can tolerate this dosage. For now, I finish my lunch, lie back, close my eyes, and allow time to evaporate, space to constrict, and for my mind to drift. I don't want to dwell on the metaphysical or existential, but I can't keep certain thoughts from dancing by and sticking to my mind, the two most common and persistent being—*What is the meaning of life?* And *I can't believe I'm going through this again.*

*   *   *

I return home, experiencing some fatigue, slight nausea, and a strange and lingering metallic taste in my mouth. But that's all I experience. The nausea goes away, I feel stronger, and so what if everything I eat tastes like aluminum foil? I'll take it, given that my last chemotherapy session landed me in the hospital for two weeks, near death. A week later, I've recovered. Five down, 13 to go. *Thirteen?* That's *all?* Insane.

With Dr. Metcalfe's okay, I move my next chemotherapy session from the upcoming Friday to the following Wednesday so I can go to Washington, D.C., for a family trip, our bottling of Bulleit for a DISCUS charity event at George Washington's historic distillery in Mount Vernon. We'll be signing and bottling 100 bottles of Bulleit Bourbon and I'll be making a short speech. I remain in constant touch with my Diageo family. I'm doing what I can, not less.

"We've got you covered here in San Francisco," Steve Beal tells me. "You take all the time you need to beat this thing, because you will."

"Thanks, Steve, and in the next couple days, if you're not doing anything and you happen to be in Grace Cathedral, replacing some candles, or wiping down the organ, or emptying the collection box, would you mind saying a prayer for me? Don't go out of your way."

"Tom, I pray for you every day, every time I step into Grace."

"Thank you. I'm glad. You're in a different time zone, so I want to make sure I have the West Coast covered. In case God sleeps in and needs a wake-up call. You never know."

"I'll be your wake-up call," Steve says. "And again, as far as work goes, we're all here, divvying everything up. We're going full-speed ahead. And know this. We'll be right here, waiting for you when you come back, ready to hand everything back to you. Just get better. Take your time. But hurry up."

What moves me is that everyone at Diageo tells me a version of what Steve says. *Get well. We've got you covered. We'll be here when you get back.* As we head up to Washington, I consider the cliché you often hear about big companies. In general, I picture them all as cold, heartless behemoths, caring only for their bottom lines and not at all for the people they employ. Diageo has shattered that image forever. I have had the opposite experience with them. The company could not be more supportive. They planned my Ambassadorship and market visits around the chemotherapy treatments and my ability to travel. I could not get through this without them.

* * *

In Washington, a flood of memories washes over me—my time on the Georgetown campus, taking classes, holing up in the law library, working in the city, walking by government buildings that awe me with their history, their stature, the energy the city exudes, the power that throbs all around me, through the air, onto the pavement, the mugginess in spring and summer that clings to you and soaks through you as if you're wearing a heavy coat. I take it all in. I allow myself to remember. That's what we have, ultimately, our memories. What we own. Then, in the afternoon, at the Diageo event at the historic George Washington distillery in Mount Vernon, I scan through my scribbled notes and talk about the history of Bulleit Bourbon.

"This is the culmination of a journey that began 150 years ago," I say, "when my great-great-grandfather Augustus emigrated from France to New Orleans, seeking his destiny in the American frontier, accepting the offer of our Founding Fathers."

I squint at my notes, and I suddenly feel frail and weak. I press on, wanting to continue my message more than I ever realized.

"My mission was to begin to pass on who we are and what we believe in, what George Washington fought for, what Augustus came here for, the fight for freedom," I say. "As it says on the Korean War Memorial, 'Freedom is not free.'"

After my speech, I help perform the ceremonial bottling and labeling of Bulleit Bourbon with Betsy, Hollis, and Tucker, sign and number labels to be auctioned off at the charity events, and then photographers descend, and I pose with the family, my smile fastened on and painful, feeling thankful for everyone here, and for only a slight tremor of nausea, this day a triumph of our product and will, until later when I look at the photos and I see Betsy smiling gamely while I stand next to her, a grinning, bony ghost.

*   *   *

I take an extra day in Washington, cramming in some sightseeing with Tucker and Betsy after the event. I stroll slowly through the Smithsonian just to soak in the magnificence and enormity of the place. I ponder the White House, the Capitol, the Washington Monument. I don't chance climbing the steps leading up to the Lincoln Memorial, but instead walk with Tucker and Betsy along the Mall that descends dramatically into the Vietnam Veterans Memorial, the plaques of the fallen rising higher and higher, finally dwarfing us with the names of the dead, listed by day, the emotion climbing into my throat. I remember moments from a speech I gave here in 1998, on Memorial Day.

"This land and its immigrants have evolved into a nation, a people, the rainbow tribe," I said, as the crowd before me went silent.

"My father was a soldier," I continued. "He served in the Second World War and lost his right eye in the Battle of the Bulge. I had a real hero and grew up playing soldier."

I outlined my own experience in Vietnam, and then I said, my voice cracking, "My old soldier is gone and I have taken his place. May I be worthy of it."

I came to the end of the speech, and I said, trying to keep my composure, "For those whose names could have been upon this wall, let us be as good in action as we are in intention. For those whose names are on this wall, let us pray."

I lowered my head and said, "Oh, Divine Master, grant that I may not try to be comforted, but to comfort, not try to be understood, but to understand, not try to be loved, but to love."

I looked up and spoke the final thought from memory, my eyes shut.

"Because it is in giving that we receive, it is in forgiving that we are forgiven, and it is in dying that we are born to eternal life."

* * *

We head home from Washington and I return to chemotherapy, the new protocol to begin at 50 percent strength of the original dose, then if I tolerate that, up to 75 percent at two-week intervals to complete my 13 remaining sessions—if all goes well.

All goes well. As Dr. Metcalfe writes, "... he tolerated week five therapy without incident...." *Without incident.* My favorite phrase. I'm doing so well that in October, I hit the road for a series of distributor presentations and holiday shows in Florida, accompanied by a doctor's note. For six days in a row, I practically live in airport terminals, taking eight flights. I feel, triumphantly—not bad. The 50 percent dose leaves me virtually without side-effects. Back from Florida, I go in for another session ... then another ... and another ... and after each one, I spend the next few days at home, recovering carefully, resting, reading, napping, taking a few phone calls, answering emails, but otherwise these days go by *without incident.* On my chart, Dr. Metcalfe practically gushes: "Overall, Thomas appears to be doing well."

Believe me, in doctor talk *that's* gushing.

* * *

I spend the fall of 2005 living in a loop of receiving chemotherapy, recovering from chemotherapy, psychologically preparing for the next chemotherapy, and taking occasional trips to work on behalf of the brand. On a Wednesday in November, I attend WhiskeyFest in New York, take the train from Penn Station to Philadelphia to attend an event held in the ballroom at the top floor of Wanamaker's Department Store, wake up at 3 a.m. Friday to take a two-connection flight from Philly to Lexington, just in time to arrive at the infusion center at St. Joseph's for my 11 a.m. chemotherapy session.

Meantime, I consult on the phone often with everyone at Diageo. The top brass sees a shift in sales, heading toward the 30,000 mark in the near future. *A nice incremental leap,* I think, *but nowhere near where we want to be, where I need to be, where I'm going to be.*

* * *

I complete the second round of chemotherapy in December, Monty having upped the dose at some point to 75 percent, with no unusual side-effects. This year, instead of sending Christmas cards, we decide to send out a holiday letter to friends and family, a letter of thanks, and a letter of Thanksgiving. As Betsy and I write the letter, chronicling the events of the year, the comings and goings of our family, and what's happening in our respective businesses, I announce, proudly, that Diageo now distributes Bulleit Bourbon in all 50 states and the media has begun to take notice. We've recently been given nice coverage in *Whisky Advocate.* I'm equally proud to announce that Betsy has reached a milestone in her career. She's completed her 25th year with Hilliard Lyons, completing 30 years in the investment industry. Betsy ends the letter by expressing our gratitude for everyone's prayers.

"We have been overwhelmed with your expression of concern, love, and compassion. They have been the foundation on which Tom and I have based his recovery."

"I like it," I say to Betsy, looking over the first draft. "Good to end on a positive note. How about wrapping it up by saying, 'This has been a great year for the Bulleits.' What do you think?"

"Tom," she says, looking past me, "this year has been a complete blur."

* * *

Third and final round of chemotherapy.

I get through the first treatment, at 75 percent, without incident. I tolerate the second treatment, feeling some fatigue and mild nausea the days after. I endure treatment three with more fatigue, more nausea, and more overall—crappiness. The fourth treatment hits me like a truck—extreme fatigue and horrendous stomach pain, nausea, diarrhea. I feel myself falling, my grip slipping, and then, wham, the side-effects demolish me. For Dr. Metcalfe's benefit, I scribble a list in the cancer journal I keep: *nausea—all the time; diarrhea—7–8 a day; stomach pain; fatigue—scale 8 of*

10; *weight loss—seven pounds; hands cracking; no appetite; C-diff could be back; generally going south.*

I see Dr. Metcalfe for an urgent follow-up. He feels that I'm heading for a possible recurrence of the infection that laid me out and landed me in the hospital for two weeks. His words gut me. I drop my head into my hands.

"Two more treatments," I mutter. "I'm about to do number *17* of the final round."

"Let's put off this treatment for another week. We'll keep the treatment at 75 percent, but let's see if we can wait out the nausea and diarrhea."

"Okay," I say, my head spinning, my stomach roiling.

"Hang in there, Tom." Then Dr. Metcalfe says quietly, "We don't want to go back to the hospital."

We.

I kind of love how he sees this as *our* cancer.

He's invested in beating this. Walking the walk right beside me.

"What happens next, Monty?" I say.

"When?"

I raise my head. "After my last treatment. After treatment six. When I beat this thing."

He shifts in his chair, clears his throat. "Well, the standard follow-up stuff. A CT/PET scan two weeks after your last treatment and then you'll have one three months after that, and then one every three months there-after. You'll need a colonoscopy every year, too."

"Okay."

We sit silently for a moment. I don't dare ask what I do if the cancer returns or, worse, if the cancer never leaves.

I mean—what *we* do.

"So let's schedule the next treatment for January 13," he says.

"Excellent. Monty, I am not going into the hospital."

Monty nods. "Good."

"And by the way—?"

I pause.

"Yes, Tom?"

"Happy New Year."

* * *

I undergo treatment number 17 of 18 overall, go home, get into bed, and wait … and wait … for the stomach pain to grip me, the nausea to roll in, for the diarrhea to attack. I hold tight for 36 hours, then 48, and— nothing. Three days later, I go to lunch with a friend who tells me I look better than I have in weeks.

"You look happier, too," he says.

"I'm on a cloud," I say. "One more treatment to go. If I get through that and I'm clear, I'll be monitored for five years and then—"

"Cancer free?"

"The doctors declare a cure. That's what they call it." I hold, smile. "I'll be bulletproof. Again."

*   *   *

The last treatment.

My final trip to the infusion center.

I receive my final infusion.

Then, home.

I wait.

Time passes.

Twenty-four hours.

Thirty-six hours.

Forty-eight hours.

Like a fighter on the ropes, defenseless, helpless, I wait to be pummeled by a series of left hooks—nausea, diarrhea, stomach cramps, fatigue, ceaseless hiccups and—nothing. I lower my guard. Waiting.

Seventy-two hours.

I gear myself up for the third-day chemo flu.

It never comes.

I go slightly south … slightly … and then it all passes.

I open my eyes and a warm, soft, golden light descends.

Hold us in Your mercy, Lord.

*   *   *

Colon cancer begins and ends, if you're lucky, with a colonoscopy and a PET/CT scan. Then, if you're remain lucky, you continue with five years of follow-up. In February, I report for my first post-surgery, post-chemo-therapy scan. I pass through the machinery, my body trapped inside a spacecraft-like cone, a procedure that would make the least claustropho-bic of us break into a sweat storm of sheer panic. I survive the scan by telling myself, over and over, "This is not the third-day chemo flu. This is a painless test. Toughen up, Tom."

And then come three days of torture, as I wait for the scan results.

On the third day after the scan, the 13th of February, a number I've always considered lucky, Dr. Metcalfe's nurse calls with the results.

"The scan shows gallstones," the nurse says, offering startling new information, explaining my most recent discomfort and yellowing skin color. "You will need to schedule an ultrasound."

"Okay, and what did the scan show for cancer?"

"Negative," the nurse says, unaware that she buried the lead.

"Negative," I whisper.

I bite my lip to stop it from trembling.

*   *   *

In March, a week before my 63rd birthday, I say goodbye to my gallblad-der, which it turns out was the cause of most of the pain I experienced. Afterward, I continue follow-up visits with Dr. Metcalfe.

"We can do every three months, or push it out to six months" he says. "That would be fine."

"Let's keep it at three," I say.

In July, after another negative scan, I receive a visit from Janet Prewitt White, Betsy's first cousin, a lawyer who gave up practicing law to attend the Lexington Theological Seminary and become the Chaplain for Hos-pice of the Bluegrass.

"How you doing, Tom?" she says.

"I'm doing well, Janet," I say. "You know, in some respects, this has been the best year of my life."

"Really? How so?"

"You see the best side of people. You see how sympathetic, empathetic, and kind people can be. You see how much they care for you and love you. It's been very deep, a very spiritual experience."

Janet nods.

"It was the drugs, Tom," she says.

Follow the Money

(You Will Find the Answers to Life's Questions Along and at the End of the Money Trail)

Revolver

MOMENTS.

A life played out in moments.

I'm vague on this exact moment.

I'm clear on the year.

2004.

Or, no, wait—2005.

Early 2005. Actually, you know what, I'm thinking 2006 …

Cancer, besides ravaging my body, distorts time.

Well, I do know this. I know the moment.

Because at that moment, everything changes.

* * *

San Francisco.

It first appears in a bar called Bruno's. The bartender responsible for this moment will soon depart for the cocktail bar of the moment, Bourbon and Branch, bringing *It* with him. After some time, the bartender leaves Bourbon and Branch and establishes his own bar, Prizefighter. By then—which would be now—the bartender and *It* have become famous.

Years later, the bartender agrees to restage the moment.

The bartender, Jon Santer, doesn't work the bar at Prizefighter. He owns it, commands it, prowling, performing like a Broadway actor—but without arrogance or aloofness. Jon remains homespun, accessible, good-natured, fun. "Hey, how you doing? Come on in, sit down, get comfortable," he says with a glance, without speaking a word.

"Hi, there. Welcome. This is my place. And this is your place. So, come on, cozy up to the bar. Great. Now, watch this. I'm going to show *It* to you. Not really that special. *It* only changed the world."

Well, changed my world, his grin says.

Changed my world, too, and modestly, *It* had a fairly large impact on the entire world of whiskey.

Jon called *It* the Revolver.

As Betsy says, game changer.

*　*　*

Behind the bar, Jon moves in staccato near-dance movements in a kind of ballet, his sturdy frame encased in a blue flannel plaid shirt, revealing two-buttons open of white tee, his brown beard cropped hipster short, his eyes twinkling and alive, his smile wide and frequent. Jon gives off a casual, tossed-off vibe as he speaks, and he moves assertively, fluid and fast. Although he's made the Revolver thousands of times, nothing feels rehearsed or tired or shrugged-off. Every move, every syllable feels real and true. Jon Santer works as a bartender, but I see an artist. And now, in front of an audience and a camera crew, he shows the world the game changer.

He claps his hands, then opens his palms like a magician preparing to do a trick.

"Okay, so I am about to make a Revolver."

He grins, and when he speaks, he tucks his tongue almost literally into his cheek. "No matter how much I kick and scream, this is the drink I will go down in history for making, for creating."

An undercurrent of agreement and applause.

Jon presses his hands together as if he's about to pray. "It's a coffee Manhattan. That's all it is." He ducks and shrugs at the patrons who fill the floor space and line the bar before him. "You guys all know that, right?"

A few people at the bar laugh. Jon roars, flicks one hand in the air in a flourish, almost like the start of a Travolta dance pose.

"That's how complex and crazy this drink is," he says, a joke.

A responding laugh from the crowd we don't see.

If this drink is so simple, I think, *I wonder why nobody else has come up with it before.*

Jon steps forward, waves his right hand, and we see he's holding a bottle of Bulleit Bourbon—label facing away from us. But you know it's Bulleit by the orange label, the golden liquid, and the shape of the bottle. By now, you have come to know Bulleit. It has become unmistakable.

Jon grabs a metal jigger with his left hand and gestures with it.

"But at the time, there weren't very many of us in San Francisco who were *making* drinks."

There it is. The explanation for why he—and he alone—invented the Revolver.

Modest, I think. *Have to love that.*

"In fact, most of us who were making drinks are in this room, right now."

He smiles, glances around the room, then seems to study the bottle of Bulleit in his hand.

"I was reacting to a lot of bespoke ingredients going around at the time."

Going against them, I think, *going against type.*

Jon chuckles, pours the Bulleit into the jigger, measuring it out, and then pours the Bulleit into a glass that looks like a beaker. *He is in a lab,* I think.

Partners in chemistry, I say, referring to bartenders.

I consider bartenders like Jon Santer as just that—chemists, in his case, a bit of magician and entertainer mixed in.

"A lot of these drinks you could only get at one bar, which I think is great," Jon says. "But at the same time, if you want a drink to really take off, you need to make it with ingredients everyone can get their hands on."

He picks up a bottle of Tia Maria, pours some into the jigger, nods, and then pours that into the beaker with the Bulleit.

"I made it with things you could find," he says. "So."

He holds up the bottle of Bulleit, flips it around, label out, facing the crowd, and the camera, and says, "This stuff had just come out. It had just launched, in 2003, I want to say."

He puts the bottle of Bulleit down on the bar and picks up the bottle of Tia Maria. "Next, a coffee liqueur. Back then we had two choices, Kahlua and Tia Maria. I like Tia Maria because it's a little more esoteric and it was rum-based. It was an ingredient that nobody had touched in, I don't know, 30 years."

He puts down the Tia Maria, surveys the bar, and says, "And then orange bitters. Coffee and orange, I think, go really well together."

He adds four ice cubes to each of the two beakers, filling both beakers at the same time with the bitters. Then he stirs the two beakers simultaneously, the clink of the ice and the whirring of the bourbon and Tia Maria sloshing, making my mouth water.

"So," he says, his voice tinged with wonder, his hands still stirring both beakers at once, "this drink has been spotted all over the world. It's in *Mr. Boston*, the cocktail book. You feel you've really made it when you make it into *Mr. Boston*."

Another laugh from the crowd. Jon stops stirring and steps to the side, showing us four extremely frosted cocktail glasses. He begins pouring the mixture from the beakers into the glasses, chuckling as he pours. "Here we are, years later, making cocktails. And now—"

He finishes pouring the cocktails into the four glasses, and then he carefully floats a slice of orange peel in each glass. Final touch. He breaks out a box of kitchen matches and lights the vapor created by the orange peels.

"*Wee*," he says, as flames shoot up from each glass.

"This looks really great in the dark," Jon adds.

"Woo!" someone shouts.

"And—Revolvers," Jon says. He steps back and spreads his arms as the customers applaud, whistle, and cheer.

Game changer.

* * *

It travels far and fast, mainly by word of mouth, what I believe always to be the most powerful way to spread the news. The Revolver becomes a *thing*. Almost immediately, the Twelve Apostles pick up the idea of the Revolver and start making them all over town. Then the Apostles' closest associates begin making Revolvers in *their* bars. Food and liquor writers discover the Revolver and write about it in publications such as *7X7*, the "in" lifestyle magazine of the Bay Area. Media outlets such as eater.com and chowhound.com spring up, becoming must reading for foodies and the new cocktail culture, touting the top places in American cities to eat, drink, date, and be seen. The media outlets write about celebrity chefs and start including bartenders, creating celebrities behind the bar, too. The sites list the hot new bars in San Francisco and promote the Bulleit Revolver as the hot new drink.

Jon Santer's travels begin. He moves to Bourbon and Branch, a dimly lit, inviting speakeasy, a place you want to be and be seen, which instantly becomes the first real cocktail bar in San Francisco, soon considered Ground Zero for the entire cocktail revolution. At Bourbon and Branch, patrons pack themselves in and watch Jon Santer work, the magician behind the bar. They see him make the Revolver. They watch him conjure this potion, a simple, delicious, dramatic drink that catches the world on fire. Literally. Jon employs the rule of three. He uses three simple ingredients and makes the cocktail in under three minutes. He ends with a flourish, sets the drink on fire. The customers ooh and ahh and applaud and everyone shouts, "What is *that?* I want one!"

It all works. The name works. The flavors work. The price point works. And most of all, the timing works. Influencers in the food and cocktail universe look west to see what's happening in the cocktail universe. They see a shining star. They see the Revolver. Within six months, 500 bars across the country put the Revolver on their menu. I keep track.

A year or so later, with Steve Beal in attendance, one of the Apostles, Erick Castro, bartender and manager at another hot San Francisco bar, the Rickhouse, creates a second Bulleit signature drink he calls the "Kentucky Buck." He also incorporates the rule of three, three ingredients—Bulleit Bourbon, ginger beer, and a generous squeeze of lemon—which he mixes in less than three minutes. Unlike the Revolver, which captures a delicious burst of flavor, an automatic palate pleaser, the Kentucky Buck is a "long drink"—cool, soothing, refreshing, meant to be savored, along the lines of a Highball or a Tom Collins.

Erick dominates his corner of the San Francisco cocktail culture, and after a while, inevitably, he receives an offer he can't refuse. He leaves the Bay Area and heads south, to San Diego, taking the Kentucky Buck with him. He soon dominates the San Diego bartender world, creates his own hit TV series, and becomes a bartender superstar. Many bartenders copy the Kentucky Buck, using Erick's idea, using other bourbons. Some claim they invented the cocktail. It doesn't matter. Erick's fame, the drink, and its name travel across the country, and around the world, eventually becoming available as far away as Australia—in a can, mixed with Bulleit Bourbon.

Then Betsy herself gets into the act. She invents a third Bulleit signature cocktail—the BLT, which stands for "Betsy's Little Treat." She employs the rule of three, in this case, Bulleit Bourbon, lemon, and tonic, all mixed in under three minutes. The BLT begins to appear on cocktail menus in bars throughout the country and we serve the BLT at our home, during Bulleit Family Trips. Everyone who tastes it touts the drink, calling it "delicious and refreshing," referring to it commonly as "The Betsy." Diageo will soon create a poster featuring the BLT or "The Betsy," that they distribute to liquor stores.

*   *   *

With the cancer appearing farther and farther in my rearview mirror, though always in the forefront of my mind, I go back to work. Hard. I hit the road, pounding the pavement, picking up where I left off. I resume my full ambassadorship duties. I meet with Diageo executives, our distributor sales people, attend Friday morning sales meetings, present to the sales force. Sometimes I present in a room of 20 people in smaller cities, say, in Little Rock; other times I present in large spaces in New York or Chicago to 220 people. I attend a string of trade conferences, WhiskyFest and Whiskies of the World in convention centers in every major city, and Tales of the Cocktail in New Orleans. And I don't forget the trade, those captains of our industry, the bartenders. I hit the hottest cocktail bars in the country. I shake every hand, from people new to the trade to bartenders I've known forever. I share laughs and tell tales on barstools and in backrooms. I put in 14-, sometimes 16-hour days and end each day feeling wasted and wake up every morning feeling energized. I'm back. I calculate that I'm on the road 150 days a year, minimum.

"Ever think of slowing down?" Steve Beal asks. Betsy knows better than to ask that.

"I can't," I say.

"Well, just a thought, given recent heath issues, maybe you should."

"What is your exit, Tom?"

"Well, death."

* * *

We do the numbers.

First, the cancer numbers.

We look at the scans every three months.

The scans read—negative, negative, negative.

Time passes, putting even more distance between me and my cancer.

Then I watch the Bulleit sales figures come in.

I pore over them three times and then I want them double-checked. Numbers don't lie, but these numbers seem incredible, totally out of whack. In what seems like a blink, we've tripled our sales. The numbers double in the next quarter … they skyrocket in the next quarter … and the next …

Ambassadorship, relationships, years in, and visionary marketing by extraordinary people.

I think of them, from the beginning until now, starting with the Brand Managers and their bosses, the Jefes: Rob Warren, heading North American Whiskey at Seagram and then at Diageo after the acquisition; Richard Nichol, who created the ambassador program; Yvonne Briese, the mother of us all; and Sophie Kelly, who navigates our current explosion to a staggering number of cases sold per year. The Jefes oversee the Brand Managers, over the years, a nine-member team of all-stars, each one all-world—Andy Johnson, who kicked us off, bringing us from acquisition and development to Seagram sales and marketing; Chris Musumeci, by my side from the moment we began at Diageo, sticking it out for six years, steering the brand's increase from 10,000 cases a year to 60,000 cases and distribution to all 50 states; Gene Song, from New York City and Seoul, a guiding star who helped establish the Family Trips; Jac Dertadian, the lady who envisioned how my ambassadorship could assist in sales and awareness; Trish Mannion, who shepherded the brand from 60,000 cases to 600,000 cases.

Trish supervised the move to the refurbished Stitzel-Weller distillery, previously the home of Old Fitzgerald and other bourbons, where, in the 1940s, Pappy Van Winkle set up shop. Some 70 years later, we take over the facility, create the Bulleit Bourbon Experience at Stitzel-Weller, and become part of the Kentucky Bourbon Trail. I move into Pappy's abandoned corner office, spruce it up, fill it with my stuff, photos, and mementos, and greet groups of visitors as they begin or end their tour of the distillery; after Trish, came Jim Ruane, who joins the team in 2012 as a junior Brand Manager, working with Trish, then moves up to Brand Manager and carries us to one million cases; Dan Levine, on whose watch we grow to 250,000 cases a year; Stephanie Jacoby, financial whiz who lobbies for and achieves a budget commensurate with a big brand; and Ed Bello, who goes from Brand Manager to Global Director of Bulleit. Call it luck, or destiny, or as I call it, once again, falling uphill, but each one of these extraordinary talents arrives bearing exactly the right skill set at exactly the right time.

It's remarkable, all of it. I remember Jim Ruane telling me, with some sense of awe and wonder, "I got the firsthand view from 200,000 to one million cases, which takes, ridiculously, only five years."

I'm no math whiz, but I call that an increase of nearly 200,000 cases—*per year*.

"Seems like we were at 6,000 cases just yesterday," someone else says. "Then, gradually, we hit a million."

"Wasn't anything gradual about it," I say. "It all just took off. Blew up. And of course, that includes the rye."

Yes.

The rye.

* * *

Some years ago, I sit on a barstool at Bourbon and Branch, Steve Beal on the stool next to me, Jon Santer on the other side of the bar, performing his magic cocktail mixtures between polishing glasses. We've come at an off hour so we can hang out with Jon before the crowds descend. And the crowds do descend. Jon has become the toast of the town, the bartender's bartender, one of the cocktail culture's main attractions. Ironically, a while ago, before the new food and whiskey revolution exploded, unsure of his future, Jon took the LSAT, thinking he might become a lawyer.

"I became a lawyer," I say. "Look where it got me."

"A life in whiskey," Jon says, laughing.

"You never know. This bourbon thing doesn't work out, I still have my law degree to fall back on."

"I've found my calling," Jon says, pouring Steve and me our drinks. He pauses in mid-pour, shakes his head, stares at us. "You know what you need to do, right?"

"Here we go," Steve says.

"What? You know what he's going to say?" I ask Steve.

"Sure, I know what he's going to say. Every bartender in town is saying it. Jon says it loudest and most often."

"Bulleit Bourbon has a large rye content," Jon says. "Many of the classic cocktails call for rye whiskey."

Jon slides us our drinks, leans in, and says to me, as if revealing the key to the secret of the universe. "Why don't you make one?"

"Maybe you should," Steve says to me, sipping his drink.

"Maybe I will."

*   *   *

I have no intention of making a rye. Jon's right, of course, Bulleit Bourbon does contain a high rye content, resulting in a drier-tasting bourbon (as opposed to a sweet bourbon), a cocktail maker's dream. I like the way things are going right now. I'm putting cancer in my rearview mirror, the bourbon has begun to take off, and I'm back on the road, logging my miles, trying to live out every day with gratitude, and loving it. The last thing I need is adding a rye whiskey to our lives.

Until I begin having conversations with Richard Nichol at Diageo. Richard, a Brit, an intellectual with a serious soccer habit—I call him a thuggish Harry Potter—is a sort of legend. He came up with the idea of the Master of Whisky program, Evan Cattanach being the first.

In the course of our conversations, Richard gently presses me to expand my vision and the brand.

"A third of our business is innovation," Richard says.

"Meaning?"

"Meaning—what is next for Bulleit?"

"Nothing. We're doing fine."

Richard keeps pressing in his gentle, persistent British way until he gives up that approach and simply says, "We are going to do something."

I start to protest and then I remember the conversation with Jon Santer over cocktails.

"Well, okay, what about a rye whiskey?"

"That's not exactly an innovation," Richard says. "That's a different category."

"I know, but we're a bar brand, and my partners in chemistry tell me rye whiskey is going to happen."

"A rye," Richard says, mulling it over. I can see his forehead crease in thought. "It is rather ... interesting."

*   *   *

Time passes. At some point later, I take a seat at the long conference table in the Diageo offices on Fifth Avenue in Manhattan. The phone call starts, we make our introductions, and someone says, "Tom, tell us about the rye."

I begin my pitch.

I tell them about my conversations with Richard Nichol.

I tell them about Jon Santer and how he asked me to make a rye for bartenders.

"Bartenders are asking for a rye," I say, my voice punched with a passion I don't expect. "Having a signature rye is something I believe in. I admit that it may be small, maybe a 10,000-cases-a-year brand, but I believe a rye will be a good thing, filling a need, finding a niche—"

I stop. I'm not loving how this is going. I pause to catch my breath, to gather my thoughts.

A hush goes through the room, spills over the telephone line.

Throats clearing, coughs, chairs scraping the floor, and then Larry Schwartz, on the phone, says, "Tom, we're not in the hobby business."

I exhale, and somehow return to my pitch, again emphasizing the value of a rye, especially for bartenders.

*   *   *

We launch Bulleit Rye in 2011. The rye has aged for seven years in new White American Oak barrels with a #4 char and consists of 95 percent rye and 5 percent malted barley. We use the same iconic bottle as the bourbon. To distinguish the rye from the bourbon, we put on a green label, again applied at a slight slant.

Bulleit Rye debuts by winning double Gold Medals for spirits and packaging at the 2011 San Francisco World Spirits Competition.

We come out with 10,000 cases. Four months later, by the summer, the demand for the rye is so great we move 40,000 cases. The demand keeps increasing. Today, Bulleit Rye has the predominant market share in the category.

I bump into Larry sometime after the launch of the rye. He grins and says, "You know, Tom, I don't make a lot of mistakes."

"You certainly don't, Larry."

"But I was wrong about that rye."

"You weren't wrong. I pitched it wrong. I thought it was going to be a small brand."

"That's true," Larry says. "You under-pitched it. So I wasn't wrong."

With a nod to Larry, I call the rye a pretty successful hobby.

Know the Facts

(There *Are* Such Things and to Know Them Is Power)

14

Vows

Standing regally on stage, Deirdre Mahlan, president of Diageo North America, leans into the microphone and says to the audience, "Join me in welcoming the founder of the Bulleit brand ... *Tom Bulleit.*"

March 14, 2017.

Shelbyville, Kentucky.

Moments later, standing on the stage next to Deirdre, overwhelmed by the enormity of it all and the ridiculousness of it all, I look over the crowd gathered before me, I find my voice once again, and I continue to speak.

"Thirty years," I say, scanning the hundreds of people sitting before me on folding chairs inside this tent on the grounds of our new—and first ever—Bulleit Bourbon distillery. Then the faces before me mesh into a kind of collage—scores of Diageo folks, members of the media, local and state politicians, my family, and friends, some who've traveled thousands of miles to celebrate this day, this momentous event, the dedication of the distillery.

"Betsy and I," I say, shaking my head, my voice cracking. I stop and then I say again, trying to process the very concept, *"Thirty years."* I pull myself together and say, "That's when we officially started our journey together. And that's when all this began. Of course, if I go back to the very beginning, when my great-great-grandfather Augustus created the original recipe for Bulleit Bourbon, we go back 170 years or so. And speaking of old, did I mention that today is my birthday?"

Applause. I bow slightly, feeling an imaginary spotlight on me burning through me and I suddenly want to wave goodbye, say a sincere thank-you. But the emotion of this moment, the emotion of all of the moments of my life seem to collide and I once again feel overcome by the enormity of this, the incredulity, and the knee-buckling gratitude that threatens to knock me over.

My one talent, as I've mentioned, has been my ability to fall uphill.

I do possess a second talent.

I seem to have a gift for surrounding myself with the absolutely best people. I have been blessed with hundreds of extraordinary partners, people who, at the least, make me look good, and at the most, have literally saved me.

And Betsy—

I find her in the front row, looking up at me, fanning herself with her program, inched forward to the edge of her folding chair, the reason in so many ways that I'm here at all, *my* reason, and I want to shout, "We made it, Betsy. Somehow. *We made it.*"

I catch her smile and I'm pulled away from this present, from this place, and I remember—our marriages.

Yes.

Marriages.

Plural.

*   *   *

Ten years ago.

New York City.

We stand outside St. Patrick's Cathedral, preparing to climb the steps leading to the massive and ornate front doors. Whenever we come to New York, Betsy and I make it a point to stop into St. Patrick's and light a candle, sit in a back pew, and say a prayer—for our children, for all those we love, for those in need, for our world. Suddenly, the doors to the majestic church fly open and dozens of elderly people, couples, men in suits or tuxedos, women in long dresses or gowns, begin making their way down the steps.

"What is this?" I ask Betsy.

She shrugs and we move over to one of the couples.

"Excuse me," I say, "what's going on in the church?"

"Fiftieth wedding anniversaries," the man says, beaming. "The Cardinal invited a whole group of us to renew our vows."

"That's wonderful," I say. "Congratulations."

I grin at Betsy. "Isn't that something?"

Betsy smiles back. "Yes. It's just what I want to do. I want to renew our vows at St. Patrick's. This year."

*   *   *

Back in Lexington, Betsy calls the Rector at Christ the King Cathedral and explains that she would like to renew our vows at St. Patrick's. The Rector, unfamiliar with such a request, promises to talk to the Bishop to figure out next steps. A week or so later, the Rector calls Betsy back.

"Mrs. Bulleit—Betsy—about renewing your vows," the Rector says.

"Yes? When can we do it?"

"We have a problem."

"What kind of problem?"

"Well, see, the thing is, you all aren't married."

Betsy pauses as she attempts to digest this insanity. "We—*what*? We have a 17-year-old *son*. We're absolutely married. I remember the wedding. I was the bride."

"Yes, no, I understand, but see, actually, you're not married. Not in the Catholic Church. So, since you're not exactly married, we can't renew your vows."

"We were *married*," Betsy says, starting to become slightly annoyed, which is one step before her becoming very annoyed, and you don't want to go *there*, "in a nondenominational church in Walnut Hill, half Episcopalian, half Presbyterian. We are obviously, clearly, 100 percent married according to civil law."

"I see where you're coming from. I do. But we have this ... issue."

Betsy, I remember, had gone through the RCIA process—the Rite of Christian Initiation for Adults—meaning she had started studying to become a Catholic. We'd decided we wanted one religion for Tucker. She finished some of the Sacraments, but then life, career, and cancer got in the way and we never finished the process, Matrimony being one of the Sacraments.

"So, what do we do?" Betsy says, swatting the ball right back into the Rector's court.

"What, ah, what do you mean?"

"I mean, what do about the renewal of our vows at St. Patrick's?"

The Rector pauses, and knowing he's overmatched, says, "I'll call the Rector at St. Patrick's."

Some days pass and the Rector calls Betsy back. "I have an answer."

"Yes?"

"The Rector at St. Patrick's said he's going to call the Canon Lawyer."

Now, at this point, you may think that this has become way too complicated and way too much of a hassle just to arrange to have our vows renewed. If you think that, you don't know Betsy.

"Good," Betsy says. "Have him call the Canon Lawyer."

Another week passes and the Canon Lawyer himself calls Betsy.

"So, Mrs. Bulleit, I've asked a bunch of people about this and here's where we are."

"Yes?"

"I don't have an answer."

"You don't have an answer?"

"No."

"Well," Betsy says, sweetly, innocently, "you need to *get* an answer."

"Okay," the Canon Lawyer says. "I have an idea. There's a guy up here who was an electrical engineer. He's about 45. He just got ordained. He became a priest two weeks ago. Why don't we leave it up to him?"

"We're coming to New York," Betsy says. "And we're going to meet him."

"Yes," the Canon Lawyer says. "Let him make the call."

We fly to New York, make an appointment with the new, very eager, very inexperienced, and very kind priest and we ask him if he will please officiate at St. Patrick's Cathedral as we renew our wedding vows.

"No," he says. "I can't do that. You have to go through all the pre-marriage steps. It's protocol. The Pre-Cana courses. You know, compatibility, making sure you understand all the ramifications, what marriage entails. It would be a marriage, understand, not a renewal."

"Father," I say, "we're already *married*. We don't need to take a course. We've been married for 20 years."

The new priest looks at me, then at Betsy.

"We already know we don't get along," Betsy says.

"Tell you what," he says. "Tom, you wait outside. I'm going to talk to Betsy for about a half hour. Then I'm going to come out and talk to you."

I wait outside St. Patrick's pacing on the steps while he talks to Betsy inside. About 10 minutes later, he walks out with Betsy, who's smiling and nodding.

"Your turn, Tom," he says to me. I follow him into his office near the front of the sanctuary. I take a seat across from him.

He has no idea what to say. He fumbles through some kind of handbook, talks about loyalty, family, and I bring up his former career in electrical engineering. He seems relieved. We talk about changing careers in midlife, we talk a little religion, I may even invite him to an upcoming Bulleit Family Trip. Finally, satisfied that Betsy and I appear to be marriage material, we go outside and find Betsy, who is standing with Tucker. He leads us back inside, down a flight of stairs to a small, stunning chapel tucked below the main sanctuary of the famous cathedral. In the chapel, his secretary greets us. She hands him some paperwork that Betsy and I sign and the secretary and Tucker co-sign as witnesses.

Then, with Tucker as our best man, photographer, and witness, with Betsy and me holding hands, the newly ordained priest marries us—in the basement, but in St. Patrick's Cathedral.

A few years later, we do actually renew our vows, this time at Grace Cathedral Church in San Francisco, with Reverend Steve Beal officiating. This time my surprise.

"This will be our third time," I remind her. "Our first wedding at Walnut Hill Church, then St. Patrick's, now Grace Cathedral."

"Third time's the charm, Tom," she says.

We enter the sanctuary at Grace, and as Father Beal leads us to a side chapel to officiate while we renew our vows, I stop and stare.

"You all moved the altar back, didn't you?"

"Yeah, we did."

"I noticed that."

"No, you didn't."

"What do you mean?"

"They moved it back in 1908, Tom."

We renew our vows. I tear up because both Betsy and Steve tear up. We go to lunch afterward, the three of us, at the Mark Hopkins Hotel, where we have stayed whenever we were in San Francisco for 30 years.

"I like renewing our vows," Betsy says.

"It's nice," I say. "Like a rebirth. Or something."

"Yes. I'm thinking we may do it again."

"Don't tell me," I say, off Betsy's look. "What are you thinking now, the Vatican?"

"What a wonderful idea, Tom. Let's look into that."

Tom, I say to myself, *on occasion, you may want to consider not speaking.* Have to work on that.

*   *   *

I stand here on the makeshift stage inside this enormous tent on the grounds of our first Bulleit distillery, in Shelbyville, moments before I will perform the ribbon cutting, wielding a monstrous pair of cartoon scissors, and again moments from my life pass before my eyes, remarkable moments, a few that I planned, many more that surprised me and that I cherish, like this one. This distillery, capable of churning out millions of gallons of whiskey, stands as a testament to our success and to my lifelong dream of becoming a bourbon distiller. I think about the circumstances and the visionaries that brought me to this place, to this stage. I think of our Brand Teams and our tireless friends at Proof Media Mix, Chuck Corcoran, Bobby Burk, and all the others. I consider the Brand's Frontier Works in collaboration with the Brand Teams and the Proof group and their creative, experiential marketing ideas, including the stunning tattoo billboard in Los Angeles, featuring 24 tattoo artists and Lisa Schulte's master work, Bulleit Bourbon, a neon billboard in Los Angeles. I recall one shining example of the Proof Media genius, a debacle that they turned into a triumph—the Bulleit Woody.

Around 2011, members of the Brand Team worked with Neiman-Marcus to create a 1930s hatch-back "camper," a trailer you could tow everywhere with a truck, complete with the luxurious leather furnishings, satellite TV, and a front end that dropped down into a bar, loaded with crystal and a year's supply of Bulleit whiskey. Neiman-Marcus offered this tricked-out Woody in their catalog as one of their Christmas "Fantasy Gifts," in the same league as some of their most outlandish items, such as an Aston-Martin personally designed by recent James Bond, Daniel Craig, available for the low, low price of $700,000, and a trip for two to Italy accompanied by your own personal chef, for a mere $200,000. The Bulleit Woody seemed like a steal at only $150,000. (It was even on *The Today Show* as a featured "fantasy gift" accompanied by Tom and Betsy.)

Unfortunately, nobody bought it. So we took the trailer to Kentucky and put it in a warehouse at Stitzel-Weller. In 2013, our Proof Media friends decided to take a chance. They brought the Woody out of retirement and parked it on the lawn at Stitzel-Weller for one of the Bulleit marketing events. Attendees flocked to the event, saw the tricked-out trailer, and went nuts. After two years in storage, the Woody became an overnight sensation. Suddenly, the brand's coolest idea became its hottest attraction. Everyone wanted to rent the Woody for their personal tailgating. As the demand grew, we discovered that one Woody just wasn't enough. The team built a duplicate—and then another. At this point, there's a fleet of Woodies, one in San Francisco, one in New York, one in Dallas, one in Chicago, and two in Louisville. The Woody has become one of Bulleit's signature marketing features, making literally thousands of appearances nationwide and in Europe.

The Woody, classic, creative, simple, and sensible, somehow makes me think of another major tenet of the Bulleit Distilling Company philosophy—*sustainability*. With a watchful, responsible eye on our environment, Bulleit has entered into a partnership with the University of Kentucky to integrate local, sustainable options in the bar program at the Visitor Experience. As a brand, Bulleit is committed to use locally sourced ingredients, support the local farming community, protect wildlife and habitats, and conserve water. The goal is to accomplish environmental sustainability and reduce the carbon footprint related to Bulleit.

The Bulleit Distilling Company has also made a commitment to sourcing 100 percent renewable energy by 2030, and is home to the first distillery solar array in our county.

I envision all this. I know what I see in the future—what I hope for—but for now, I must say I have trouble imagining what comes next, beyond this makeshift stage, beyond this event. It boggles my mind to imagine that two years from now, in 2019, Diageo would break ground on a new, mega Diageo distillery capable of producing 10 million proof gallons of whiskey. The Bulleit brand will continue expanding, too, into Europe and Asia. The point is, Bulleit keeps going, charging forward, eyes on the future, with a deep and sincere appreciation of the past. But at this moment, I take a deep breath, step away from the podium, grab the huge joke scissors with both hands, and cut into the foot-wide red ribbon that flaps leisurely in front of me. I laugh, the applause of the hundreds standing before me, the sound covering me like a warm wave.

Is this a dream? I wonder.

* * *

"It's a dream," Betsy says.

"What part?"

"All of it."

We're sitting on the porch of our inn at Martha's Vineyard, where we've taken a few days to decompress, to recharge, to not, I've been assured, renew our vows, at least not yet. Six months before, Diageo had announced its intention to build a second Kentucky distillery, where Bulleit would be made. Sometimes this all feels insane, impossible, surreal.

"You know, Tom, I've been thinking," Betsy says. "You have achieved your biggest success after the age of 70."

"You're right about that. What does that say about me? Probably that I'm a slow learner."

She ignores me. "I heard a story once. Three people start their own businesses at the same time. They are equally talented, equally intelligent, and equally funded. But only one will succeed. You know why?"

"Because the other two will quit."

She peers at me over her sunglasses, smiles, and gives me a look that says, *Well, obviously, you would know the right answer to that question.*

I raise my glass to my wife.

We toast, clink glasses, and look off toward a future of more dreams, and vows, and moments, watching the evening sun fade.

Focus on the Task at Hand

(If You Don't Complete What You're Doing Right Now, Nothing Comes Next)

Finally

SO THAT'S IT, all I've got, the small story of a life, my life, such as it is, a tale of deep faith, unyielding commitment, falling uphill, nearly dying—twice—learning from others and sharing what I've learned, and ultimately offering an insight into being an entrepreneur, a testament that you have to be a little crazy, pathologically passionate, acknowledge the fear, see it, own it, and never allow the fear to get in your way. And like every successful entrepreneur, you have to bet on your own hunch. Push your entire stack of chips in front of you—with confidence, even if you're bluffing, which you no doubt will be—and go all in. That's what I did. That's what you have to do. Finally, make it personal and make it last. Don't build it for yourself. Build it for your grandchildren.

And you thought this was going to be about bourbon, didn't you?

Bulleit Points

Rules and Observations of Making It in Business … and in Life

Be Proactive
(Problems Do Not Resolve Themselves)

* * *

Presume Nothing
("No, This Gun Isn't Loaded")

* * *

Be Prepared
(Embrace the Wisdom of the Boy Scouts)

* * *

If It Doesn't Seem Right, It Probably Isn't
(Trust Your Gut)

* * *

20/40/60
(At 20, You Worry Yourself Sick About What People Think of You.

At 40, You Say, "The Hell with 'Em."

At 60, You Realize They Were Not Thinking About You.)

* * *

Go All In
(Without Commitment and Passion—Which Are Infectious—*It* Won't Happen)

* * *

Be Afraid
(Today May Be the Day It All Turns to Shit)

* * *

Make It Personal
(We Are All in the Relationship Business)

* * *

"No battle was ever won by spectators."
—John Le Carré

* * *

Be Result Oriented
(Nothing Was Built by Performing Tasks)

* * *

Find Humility Before It Finds You
(Life Is Coming to Get Us All)

* * *

Plan Ahead
(If You're in the Far-Left Lane and You Need to Exit Right in 500 Feet, You May Arrive in the Afterlife Instead of Altoona)

* * *

No News Is Not Good News
(Things Are Just Getting Worse)

* * *

Follow the Money
(You Will Find the Answers to Life's Questions Along and at the End of the Money Trail)

* * *

Know the Facts
(There *Are* Such Things and to Know Them Is Power)

* * *

Focus on the Task at Hand
(If You Don't Complete What You're Doing Right Now, Nothing Comes Next)

* * *

Don't Just Design the Aesthetic, Build It. Execution Is Everything.

* * *

Performance of a Skill Does Not Require Flawless Execution, But Rather Fewer Misses Than Most

* * *

Try to Find a Way to Become Un-Lonely

* * *

Nothing Quite Validates a Statistic Like Its Aberration

* * *

We Remember What We Want to Forget and Forget What We Want to Remember

* * *

If You Can Get from There to Here, You Can Get from Here to There. Success Is Not an Arrival. It Is a Platform for the Next Step.

* * *

"Rule number one of survival: Never, never tell anyone what you really think."
—Edward Rutherford

* * *

"It is with literature as with law or empire— an established name is an estate in tenure, or a thrown-in possession."
—Edgar Allen Poe

* * *

"A bit of money makes all the difference."
—Jane Gardam

* * *

"Perfection is achieved not when there is nothing left to add, but when there is nothing left to take away."
—Antoine de Saint-Exupery

* * *

"In order to attain the impossible, one must attempt the absurd."
—Miguel de Cervantes

* * *

You Can Live Lamenting the Past, or Imagine a Bright Future by Simply Flipping the Switch in Your Head. Change the Channel.

* * *

I Have Been Extraordinarily Blessed in the Prayers God Has Answered and in Those Un-Answered

* * *

And Finally, from My Mother-in-Law: "With every step forward we leave something behind, and what is found is often not as valuable as what is lost."
—Rosemary Codell Brooks

Acknowledgments

So as not to leave anyone unmentioned, I would like to express this universal acknowledgment and expression of gratitude to the thousands of people who have produced, marketed, and sold the Bulleit Brands. It is truly your Brand and your Distillery. And to all our family and friends who have encouraged us over the many years. And Alan, and Bobbie for putting up with Alan. Eve Attermann, our, Alan and Tom's, marriage broker. And Wiley, who knew a sure thing when they saw it.

About the Author

IN 1987, THOMAS E. BULLEIT, JR., fulfilled a lifelong dream of reviving an old family bourbon recipe by starting the Bulleit Distilling Company. He has since forged a name for himself within the whiskey industry, including election to the Kentucky Bourbon Hall of Fame in 2009. Bulleit Bourbon continues to receive accolades within the spirits industry, specifically Gold and Double Gold medals at the San Francisco World Spirits Competition.

Tom earned his B.A. from the University of Kentucky in 1966. He is a Vietnam veteran and served with the First Marine Division from 1967 to 1969. Upon returning home, Tom earned his law degree from the University of Louisville School of Law and an advanced law degree (LL.M.) from the University of Georgetown, while he practiced with the U.S. Department of the Treasury. He moved to Lexington, Kentucky, and co-founded the law firm Bulleit, Kinkead, Irvin, and Reinhardt.

Continuing the legacy and success of Bulleit Bourbon, Tom launched Bulleit Rye Whiskey in 2011. Bulleit Rye has earned both Double Gold and Gold at the San Francisco Spirits Competition.

Bulleit 10-Year was added to the family in 2013. Most recently, Bulleit Barrel Strength became the newest award-winning whiskey to join the portfolio in 2016. Bulleit Barrel Strength was named Best Straight Bourbon and awarded a Double Gold medal at the 2018 San Francisco World Spirits Competition.

Construction began on the Bulleit Distilling Co. in Shelbyville, Kentucky, in 2014. The distillery opened with an official ribbon-cutting event on March 14, 2017, during which Bulleit's 30th anniversary was also celebrated, as well as his 30th wedding anniversary.

In 2019, the Bulleit Distilling Co. opened its doors to the public with the launch of a state-of-the-art Visitor Center.

Always a bartender favorite, Bulleit Bourbon was announced as the bestselling and most trending American Whiskey brand in the world's best bars, according to the Drinks International Brand Report, for the fourth consecutive year.

Tom is married to Elizabeth Calloway Brooks, who was named after her ancestor, Elizabeth Callaway, Daniel Boone's niece. They have two children, Hollis and Tucker. As a Louisville native, Tom was named a Hometown Hero in 2014 as the program's 22nd inductee. He also received the Martin G. Hanse, Sr., Humanitarian Award in 2016 from the Marine Corps Coordinating Council of Kentucky.

Index